天津市哲学社会科学规划课题（TJZWQN18-003）

汉语分裂句的信息结构研究
Cleft Sentences in Chinese: An Analysis from the Perspective of Information Structure

郑丹阳 著

南开大学出版社
NANKAI UNIVERSITY PRESS

天 津

图书在版编目(CIP)数据

汉语分裂句的信息结构研究 / 郑丹阳著. —天津：南开大学出版社，2025.2
ISBN 978-7-310-06560-8

Ⅰ.①汉… Ⅱ.①郑… Ⅲ.①汉语－句法－研究 Ⅳ.①H146.3

中国国家版本馆 CIP 数据核字(2023)第 233900 号

版权所有　侵权必究

汉语分裂句的信息结构研究
HANYU FENLIEJU DE XINXI JIEGOU YANJIU

南开大学出版社出版发行
出版人：王　康
地址：天津市南开区卫津路 94 号　　邮政编码：300071
营销部电话：(022)23508339　营销部传真：(022)23508542
https://nkup.nankai.edu.cn

天津泰宇印务有限公司印刷　全国各地新华书店经销
2025 年 2 月第 1 版　　2025 年 2 月第 1 次印刷
230×155 毫米　16 开本　14 印张　2 插页　222 千字
定价：68.00 元

如遇图书印装质量问题，请与本社营销部联系调换，电话:(022)23508339

Preface

This book presents a systematic and comprehensive study of Chinese cleft sentences from the perspective of information structure. The term "cleft sentence" in Chinese refers to a syntactic structure primarily taking the form of "shi ... de", which realizes the focusing function by placing the focus constituent in a more prominent syntactic position (specifically, following the focus marker "shi"). Unlike their English counterparts, Chinese cleft sentences can be understood as "information-driven" cleft sentences, meaning to "cleave" the canonical sentences into two informative segments, namely presupposition and focus, from the perspective of information structure.

In this book, the criteria of cleft constructions are established through a multidisciplinary perspective, encompassing semantics, pragmatics and information structure, to distinguish Chinese cleft constructions from the non-cleft "shi ... de" sentences with similar surface structures. Besides, departing from the analysis of their information structure, the properties of Chinese cleft sentences are explored through the following investigations. Firstly, an analysis of the categorization of Chinese cleft sentences are conducted from the types of focus structures. Secondly, the configurations of the informational components (namely focus, topic, presupposition) in different types of Chinese cleft sentences are examined. Lastly, an investigation is made into how the components of the information structure are conveyed through both mental representations (i.e., identifiability) as well as grammatical forms.

To ensure the authenticity and objectivity of the results, the data for the present study are drawn from two authoritative online corpora: the Center for Chinese Linguistics Corpus at Peking University (hereafter referred to as CCL) and the Beijing Language and Culture University Corpus Center (hereafter referred to as BCC).

The theoretical framework underpinning this study is grounded in Lambrecht's (1994) theory of information structure, which encompasses key components such as focus structure typology, the Topic Acceptability Scale, and the model of identifiability, among others. Additionally, Chen's (2004) exploration of the correlation between identifiability and definiteness in the Chinese language serves as another crucial theoretical support for this study. A novel model of identifiability is developed based on the theories of Lambrecht (1994) and Chen (2004), aligned with the language examples presented in this study.

Zheng Danyang
August, 2023
Tianjin University, China

List of Abbreviations

1SG — first-person singular

2SG — second-person singular

3SG — third-person singular

ACC — accusative

AdvP — adverbial phrase

AP — adjective phrase

CL — classifier

COMP — complementizer

CONJ — conjunction

COP — copula

DAT — dative

DEF — definite article

DE_{modi} — modifier marker "de"

DE_{nomi} — nominalizer "de"

DE_{poss} — possessive marker "de"

DE_{ptcl} — particle "de"

EXPL — expletive pronoun

GEN — genitive

IMP — imperfect tense verb

LE_{aspc} — aspect marker "le"

LOC — locative

MOD — modal

N — noun
NMLZ — nominalizer
NOM — nominative
NP — nominal phrase
OBJ — object
PFV — perfective
PP — prepositional phrase
PREP — preposition
PRT — particle
PST — past tense
PTCP — past participle
Q — question particle
REL — relative pronoun
SC — small clause
SHI_{aux} — auxiliary verb "shi"
SHI_{cop} — copular verb "shi"
SUBJ — subject
TOP — topic marker
V — verb
VP — verb phrase

Contents

Chapter 1 Introduction 1

    1.1   The Scope of This Study 3
    1.2   Research Objectives 6
    1.3   Research Questions 9
    1.4   Research Hypothesis 10
    1.5   Structure of the Book 10

Chapter 2 An Overview of Cleft Sentences 12

    2.1   Cleft Sentences in English 13
    2.2   Cross-linguistic Perspectives on Cleft Sentences 24
    2.3   Summary 35

Chapter 3 Cleft Sentences in Chinese 36

    3.1   Forms of Chinese Cleft Sentences 38
    3.2   Classifications of Chinese "shi … de" Sentences 39
    3.3   Semantic and Functional Properties of Chinese Cleft Sentences 45
    3.4   The Syntactic and Functional Role of "shi" in Cleft Sentences 61
    3.5   The Syntactic and Functional Role of "de" in Cleft Sentences 66

3.6 Summary 68

Chapter 4 Theoretical Framework 71

4.1 Information Structure: An Overview 71
4.2 Focus Types and the Configuration of the Information
    Structure 86
4.3 Identifiability, Referentiality, and Definiteness 92
4.4 Identifiability and Activation in Discourse 98
4.5 Cognitive Perspective on Identifiability 106
4.6 Summary 108

Chapter 5 Methodology and Data Collection 110

5.1 Data Source 111
5.2 Data Extraction 112
5.3 Criteria for Data Selection and Analysis 116
5.4 Classification and Sorting Procedure 127

**Chapter 6 Grammatical and Informational Interpretations
    of Cleft Foci** 132

6.1 Focus Domains and Types of Focus Structures 133
6.2 Syntactic Categories of Focus Constituents 143
6.3 Grammatical Categories of Nominal Phrases in Focus
    Domains 144
6.4 Discussion and Summary 156

Chapter 7   The Identifiability of the Focus and Topic Constituents in Chinese Cleft Sentences 162

7.1 The Distribution of Focus and Topic Constituents Across Identifiable Statuses 162
7.2 Identifiability of Focus and Topic Constituents in Argument-cleft Sentences 166
7.3 Identifiability of Focus and Topic Constituents in Adjunct-cleft Sentences 168
7.4 Grammatical Expressions and Their Identifiability Status 173
7.5 The Markedness of Chinese Cleft Sentences from the Perspective of Focus Typology 185
7.6 Summary 187

Chapter 8   Conclusion 190

8.1 Chinese Cleft Sentences and Chinese "shi … de" Sentences 190
8.2 Types of Chinese Cleft Sentences and the Grammatical Categories of Focus/Topic Constituents 192
8.3 Identifiability of Focus and Topic Constituents 193
8.4 Theoretical and Practical Contribution 193
8.5 Limitations and Future Research Directions 194

References 196
In Memory of Professor Yan Huang 213

Chapter 1

Introduction

As in many other non-English languages, the concept of cleft sentences in Chinese originated from cleft sentences in English. However, considering the typological differences across languages, it is obvious that the syntactic criteria of cleft sentences in English cannot be directly applied to Chinese or other languages. In other words, the syntactic criteria of cleft sentences in English lack typological significance in solving cross-linguistic issues.

The cleft sentence in Chinese is meant the syntactic structure mainly holding the form of "是……的 (shi ... de)" and realizing the function of focusing by puttting the focus constituent in a syntactically more prominent position (i.e., the following position of the focus marker "shi"), and by "cleaving" the cannonical proposition into two segments (i.e., presupposition and focus) from the perspective of information structure.

From a syntactic perspective, Chinese cleft sentences differ from their English counterparts in terms of the generative movement of constituents. Chinese cleft sentences generate the focus by inserting the focus marker "是 (shi)" at the preposition of the constituent the speaker aims to highlight, keeping the rest of the sentence in situ. From an information structure perspective, both English and Chinese cleft sentences achieve the function of focusing by presupposing and splitting the information conveyed by canonical propositions. Therefore, the definition, classification, and analysis of cleft sentences from the perspective of information structure have a more unified standard cross-linguistically. The informational departure of this book also aligns with Professor Lu Jianming's proposal of establishing a new "exploration path" for Chinese grammar research from the perspective of language information structure (Lu, 2018, p. 163).

Different from traditional studies, which provide classifications of "shi ... de" sentences mainly from grammatical categories of "shi" and "de", this book provides a general standard for cleft structures from semantics, pragmatics, and information structure perspectives, intending to construct a mechanism to distinguish Chinese cleft sentences from other non-cleft "是……的 (shi ... de)" sentences.

This research also closely examines the following characteristics of Chinese cleft sentences from the following perspectives of information structure: firstly, the mechanisms of information delivery in Chinese cleft sentences — in other words, what is the configuration of information structure (i.e. focus, topic and presupposition) for different sentence structures realizing various functions; and secondly, how does the information conveyed successfully through referentiality and identifiability of its informational constituents?

In terms of the research methodology, this study is a corpus-based qualitative research. The empirical data comes from the CCL and BCC corpora.

The theoretical foundation of this study is Lambrecht's (1994) information structure theory, including the identifiability model and the relevant discussions about focus types, among others. Through the analysis of empirical Chinese data, necessary supplements and modifications to the theoretical model are made to better adapt to the typological features of Chinese cleft sentences. The research findings, such as the semantic, informational, and functional features of Chinese cleft sentences; as well as the criteria for distinguishing them from non-cleft "shi...de" sentences, offer theoretical support for the language research of Chinese clefts. Additionaly, these findings hold pedagogical importance to Chinese teaching, especially for teaching Chinese as the second language.

1.1 The Scope of This Study

Cleft sentences are widely-used syntactic constructions that give prominence to the constituent (considered as the "focus") the speaker aims to highlight in conversation or discourse. Normally, cleft sentences are used to indicate contrast to highlight the "focused" constituent.[①] To give prominence to the "focused" constituent, the sentence or proposition is divided into two parts from an informative perspective if the syntactic partition is not significantly noticeable in some languages.

The concept of the cleft sentence was put forward and named with respect to the study of English (Jespersen, 1927). Since then, it has been gradually accepted and applied to many languages (see Kizu, 2005; Lee, 2005; Paul and Whitman, 2008). Despite the theoretical development in this area cross-linguistically, one unavoidable problem still exists — how does the same concept adjust to and apply to different languages, albeit the significant syntactic distinctions between languages? Considering the similar functions of cleft sentences that may be realized in different languages, we assume that there must be some standard criteria not influenced by language differences that we can resort to when judging cleft sentences.

English is very rich in cleft sentences. The main form of the English cleft sentence[②] is "It BE ... that/WH-", with the constituent after BE as the "focus" of the sentence, and the "that-" or "WH-clause" expressing the old information known by both the speaker and listener called "presupposition"

---

① English cleft sentences are often considered to be structures that function to express contrastive focus (see Drubig, 2003), but researchers of cleft sentences in other languages still insist that the communicative functions of foci of cleft sentences in their language are different from that in English cleft sentences.

② English cleft sentences are classified into different types. The most accepted classification is given by Collins (1991a)—cleft sentences (equal to IT-cleft); pseudo-cleft sentences, which are subdivided into wh-clefts and th-clefts; and reversed pseudo-cleft sentences. In this study, the term "cleft sentence" is used to refer to the first type (i.e., IT-cleft sentences) in all languages (i.e., English, Chinese, and other mentioned languages). To avoid any misunderstanding caused by the dummy subject "it", I avoid the term "IT-cleft" sentence.

in pragmatics.

According to Collins' (1991a) corpus-driven study, in addition to cleft sentences, English exhibits two other major structural variants used for focus construction — pseudo-cleft sentences and reversed pseudo-cleft sentences. These constructions are typically realized through the patterns "what … BE (that/WH-)" and "(that/WH-) BE what … ", respectively, wherein the focused constituent is embedded within the "that" or "wh-" clause. Functionally and semantically speaking, English cleft sentences are structures aiming to place "focus" syntactically in a highlighted position of a sentence beyond the "presupposed" proposition. In English, multiple linguistic strategies can be employed to convey focus. Noncanonical focus, for instance, can be delivered by methods of information packaging such as preposing, clefts, inversions, and so on (Prince, 1981). From the perspective of information structure, the cleft sentence represent a marked syntactic construction employed to highlight the focus of a proposition.

The introduction of the term "cleft sentences" within English linguistics has prompted scholars to investigate the presence and typological equivalents of such constructions in other languages. Based on native speakers' intuition, English cleft sentences are "translated" into corresponding structures in other Indo-European languages that are syntactically similar to their English counterparts. For example, the structures "Er sein … , de … " in German and "C'est … qui … " in French are syntactically like the English cleft sentence. Intuitively, native speakers would translate English clefts into these two forms in German and French, respectively. However, scholars have raised concerns regarding the correlation between the communicative function and the syntactic structure of the translated counterparts.

Considering the functional dimension, scholars across various languages have examined whether the translated equivalents in their respective languages can be classified as cleft sentences. In other words, they have explored whether the functional and semantic properties of these translated structures align with those of English cleft constructions. Positive and negative opinions merged. To take one example, Lambrecht (1994) proposed that French cleft sentences are legitimate and nearly equivalent to those of English; however, Clech-Darbon et al. (1999) took the opposite idea — they stated that there are, in fact, no real cleft sentences per se in French.

It is widely-accepted that Chinese cleft sentences typically take the form of "shi ... de", where the constituent following "shi" — usually a nominal or adverbial phrases — functions as the sentence's focus and is often prosodically stressed. In the case of pseudo-clefts, the structure "……的是……(... de shi ...)" where "de" introduces a nominal clause and the preceding element commonly appears as a verb phrase, is widely recognized by Chinese scholars (cf. Fang, 1995; Huang and Fawcett, 1996, etc.). The following two sentence are typical examples of the Chinese cleft sentence.

(1-1) 我是**昨天**[1] 来北京的。
Wǒ shì zuótiān lái Běijīng de.
1SG SHI$_{aux}$ yesterday come to Beijing DE$_{ptcl}$.
It was **yesterday** that I came to Beijing.

(1-2) 是**小明**打小华的。
Shì Xiǎomíng dǎ Xiǎohuá de.
SHI$_{aux}$[2] Xiaoming hit Xiaohua DE$_{ptcl}$.
It was **Xiaoming** who hit Xiaohua.

Existing literature has predominantly examined the syntactic and semantic properties of Chinese cleft sentences, while comprehensive investigations into their information structure remain relatively scarce to date.

---

[1] In the illustrative examples, the bolded words and expressions indicate the focus constituents within the respective sentences.

[2] This study posits that in Chinese cleft sentences, "shi" acts syntactically as an auxiliary, exhibiting distinct syntactic properties compared to its occurance in other structurally similar constructions, such as "shi" copula sentences in Chinese. A detailed analysis of the syntactic and functional classes and properties is presented in Chapter 3.

1.2 Research Objectives

While English cleft sentences have been studied from perspectives of forms and functions, relevant Chinese studies are mainly lingering in the discussions concerning cleft sentences' syntactic forms and properties. As essential means of information packaging, cleft sentences need to be investigated pragmatically in discourse.

From the perspective of information structure, Chinese cleft sentences are marked constructions expressing focus meanings by deliberately partitioning unmarked sentence structures into two segments. By uttering the cleft sentences, speakers establish the relationship between given and new information by providing the possible presupposition shared by both the speaker and the hearer and the exhaustive set of possible focus items. Pragmatically, the use of the cleft sentences reflects the speaker's assessment of the hearer's knowledge and perception.

The primary focus of this study is the information structure of Chinese cleft sentences, which refers to the organization and presentation of information within communication or text. The information structure involves the way speakers or writers convey the content of their message to their audience. The way information is structured in a text or speech significantly influences its comprehensibility and retention by listeners. An effectively organized information structure enhances the audience's ability to identify the central message and recall key details.

This study examines the configuration of information structure in Chinese cleft sentences and other "shi...de" constructions, employing it as a key criterion to differentiate Chinese "shi...de" cleft sentences from other "shi...de" sentence types. Additionally, it explores the relationship between sentence functions and information structure, examining the transimission of information and the cohesive organization of discourse. Specially, the study analyzes how information progresses from old to new and how presupposition, focus, and assertion interact within the sentence.

It is important to note that although this study is not a comparative study between Chinese and any other languages, English is still considered the point of reference because of its prominent influence in this field. Several studies on Chinese cleft sentences have been conducted within a contrastive framework, comparing Chinese with English. Given the influence of English-based analyses, researchers often find it difficult to examine Chinese cleft constructions without reference to English. However, as fundamentally distinct linguistic systems, Chinese and English exhibit structural and functional differences that, in many respects, limit their direct comparability. For example, syntactically, the English clefts and pseudo-clefts are formed by syntactic movements, such as wh-movement (Akamjian, 1970); however, for Chinese clefts, there is no such movement in the process. Considering the differences in the syntactic structures between English and Chinese constituents, cross-linguistic studies conducted from the perspective of syntax will be less practical.Instead, by adopting information structure as the analytical framework, the focus shifts to the effective transmission and reception of information as a pragmatic and functional unit. While the primary concern is the information structure of Chinese cleft sentences, the analysis remains grounded in an initial examination of their syntactic forms to ensure a comprehensive and systematic approach.

The data used in this study are collected from two online Chinese corpora. To ensure objectivity, this study incorporates texts from various genres, representing both formal and informal discourse, to achieve a balanced dataset. However, two important considerations must be noted. First, the distributional variation of cleft sentences across different genres is not the primary focus of this study; rather, the selection of diverse texts serves solely to enhance data balance and analytical neutrality. Second, oral data, such as those from audio corpora, are not included due to practical constraints in collecting a sufficient and accessible dataset. Additionally, in spoken communication, the primary function of cleft constructions —

focus marking — can often be achieved through alternative means, such as prosodic prominence on the intended focus constituent, thereby reducing the necessity for cleft structures. This possible phenomenon can be explained by the economic principle of language.[①] In this regard, information structures realize their pragmatic functions by various means, e.g., morphologically, syntactically, phonologically, and so on. If the same function can be reached through the phonological method in the process of communication (especially for languages in which phonetic factors greatly influence meaning), the usage of syntactic methods would be optionally reduced depending on the context. In contrast, within written contexts where prosodic cues are unavailable, authors are compelled to rely on syntactic strategies to fulfill pragmatic functions such as focus marking. This necessity effectively excludes the influence of phonological variables, thereby highlighting the role of syntactic constructions — such as clefts — as primary vehicles for encoding information structure in written discourse. While this study does not address the prosodic features that distinguish Chinese cleft sentences, it acknowledges that prosody plays a crucial role in the realization of information structure. Prosodic cues function as integral means of highlighting focus and conveying pragmatic intent, and their interaction with syntactic and semantic structures may vary across different sentence types.

In the process of data collection and selection, certain criteria must be used to retrieve the relevant data and exclude the superficially similar but non-qualifying data. After the initial automatic search, all the data were thoroughly examined according to the criteria listed and outlined in Chapter

---

[①] As a tenet or tendency shared by all living organisms, the concept of the economy may be referred to as "the principle of least effort." It explains humans' tendency to achieve the maximum result with the minimum amount of effort that is necessary. Being a biological principle at the very beginning stage, this phenomenon has been found in the linguistic field by scholars such as Whitney (1877), Sweet (1888), Leopold (1930), and Zipf (1949). Martinet (1955) provided a comprehensive definition of the linguistic economy as the unstable balance between the needs of communication-which are always changing-and natural human inertia, two essential forces contributing to the optimization of the linguistic system.

5. The ones that do not satisfy any of the criteria will be excluded from the selection procedure.

This qualitative, corpus-based study builds upon and extends previous research by incorporating empirical data. Unlike earlier studies that primarily relied on introspective examples, the use of corpus data in this study ensures a more evidence-based analysis, enhancing the reliability and validity of the findings.

1.3 Research Questions

For many scholars in the field of pragmatics, information structure is understood as a phenomenon that operates across both sentence-level constructions and broader discourse-level frameworks (see Roberts, 1996).

Therefore, this study starts from the sentence-level construction — the Chinese cleft sentence; and investigates how the information structure works in the discourse by observing and analyzing its distributions and configurations. The following questions will be discussed.

(i) What are the semantic and informational criteria that define cleft sentences in Chinese? How can they be distinguished from other non-cleft "shi ... de" sentences?

(ii) How can "shi...de" sentences be classified, and what are their distinct semantic and pragamtic charactersitics ?

(iii) What are the syntactic categories of focus constituents in Chinese cleft sentences?

(iv) How are the focus and topic elements of Chinese cleft sentences be accessed? Is there a hierarchical degree of identifiability among different constituents? Furthermore, what is the relationship between the identifiability of grammatical forms and informational constituents, such as focus and topic?

1.4 Research Hypothesis

Considering the research questions of the present study, I list the following hypotheses here as the tentative interpretations as well as the guidance of the study.

(i) The syntactic properties of English clefts cannot be applied directly to Chinese. Instead, it is necessary to establish semantic and informational criteria specifically tailored to the analysis of Chinese cleft sentences.

(ii) Regarding the types of focus structures, Chinese cleft sentences may hold different forms of focus.

(iii) Argument or subject of the sentence being the focus constituent is a common phenomenon in Chinese cleft sentences.

(iv) As important components of information structure, "presupposition" and "focus" exhibit distinct features in Chinese cleft sentences compared to other non-cleft "shi … de" sentences. Moreover, the structural configurations of presupposition, focus, and assertion differ between Chinese cleft sentences and their non-cleft "shi … de" counterparts.

(v) In Chinese cleft sentences, focus constituents serve as carriers of new information and are typically realized through indefinite or unidentifiable expressions, which convey non-uniqueness and non-specificity.

1.5 Structure of the Book

The remaining content of this book is organized as follows.

In Chapter 2 and 3, previous researches based on cleft sentences are elaborated across languages. Among different languages, English clefts, as the initiation of the cleft sentence studies, and Chinese clefts, being the objectives of the present study, are examined in detail.

Chapter 4 provides an overview of the theoretical framework underlying this study, along with a discussion of its conceptual development and evolution. This study examines key concepts such as "presupposition" "assertion" "focus", which realize the process of meaning-delivery as a combination of pieces of information. Additionally, it explores "identifiability" and "definiteness", which encode how the syntactic constituents are valued on aspects of (cognitive) perception (of both speaker and listener) and grammatical manifestation. Chinese cleft sentences are analyzed at these two levels to derive insights into their distinctive charactersitics in information transmission within cleft sentences.

Chapter 5 outlines the primary research methods and procedural steps, detailing the criteria for data selection and the exclusion of non-qualifying samples.

Chapter 6 provides a detailed discussion of the grammatical and informational features of foci of Chinese cleft sentences. To understand how clefts deliver information, the connections between syntactic constituents of the clefts (i.e., of their focus and topic constituents) and their identifiability are established. The data collected from the corpora are checked from the perspectives of the syntactic structure of their focus constituents and their definite/ indefinite reference. The relationship between the focus constituent and the definiteness/indefiniteness of its NP is also discussed from the perspective of information structure.

Chapter 7 examines the identifiability of the focus, topic constituents based on the integrated model of identifiability proposed in the study. By analyzing the identifiability of various grammatical forms (e.g., personal pronouns, bare nouns), this study seeks to evaluate the applicability of the acceptability scale for topics proposed by Ariel (1990) and Lambrecht (1994) in the context of Chinese cleft sentences. Furthermore, it aims to establish a systematic account of the identifiability patterns of focus constituents in Chinese cleft constructions.

In Chapter 8, a summary of the findings, the significance and limitations of the study are presented.

Chapter 2

An Overview of Cleft Sentences

Following the studies of English cleft sentences, the studies of their counterparts extend from language to language. Studies of cleft sentences in English are well-formed and consist of diverse opinions from various perspectives. Studies of cleft sentences in Chinese mainly discuss the following four problems: the forms of cleft sentences in Chinese (see Cheng, 2008; Fang, 1995; Hashimoto, 1969; Huang and Fawcett, 1996; Paul and Whitman, 2008; Song, 1978; Teng, 1979; Wang, 1944); the syntactic classes of "shi" and "de" in Chinese cleft sentences (see Chiu, 1993; Chu, 1979; Hashimoto,1969; Huang, 1982; Li and Thompson, 1981; Ross, 1983; Shi, 1994; Simpson and Wu, 1999; Tang, 1983; Teng, 1979; Xu and Li, 1993; Zhu, 1978); the functions of Chinese cleft sentences (see Cheng, 2008; Hole, 2011); and, albeit to a lesser extent, the information structure of cleft sentences in Chinese (see Hole, 2013).

As a linguistic phenomenon, the cleft sentence has been gaining much attention from linguists for its (contrastive) focus function delivered in the sentence. The discussion of the cleft sentence not only stimulates the development of the theoretical principles of this sentence but also offers a typological topic for studies of different languages. In this chapter, I will review the previous studies to pave the way for the present study.

2.1 Cleft Sentences in English

2.1.1 Definition

Like many other linguistic terms, the definition of cleft sentences has evloved over time. The following are several definitions of the "it-cleft", cited from Calude (2007).

(i) Quirk et al. (1985, p. 951): "(The cleft sentence is) a special construc- tion which gives both thematic and focal prominence to a particular element of the clause […] so-called [cleft sentences] because it divides a single clause into two separate sections, each with its own verb."

(ii) Sornicola (1991, p. 4638): "(Cleft sentences are) defined by the 'clefting pattern ' 'be+NP+S', where the NP is focused and in English, one also finds the dummy it."

(iii) Bussmann (2000, p.76): "Cleft/ pseudo-cleft sentences are syntactic constructions where a single clause has been divided into two clauses. 'clefting' refers to the transformation in generative transformational grammar, which derives the cleft sentence from the basic construction. Cleft/ pseudo-cleft sentences serve to mark the constituents that are the focus of the sentence and are primarily used to indicate contrast."

(iv) Lambrecht (2001, p.467): "Cleft sentence is defined more comprehensively, from a structural as well as pragmatic standpoint as a complex sentence structure consisting of a matrix clause headed by a copula and a relative or relative-like clause whose relativized argument is coindexed with the predicate-argument of the copula. Taken together, the matrix and the relative express a logically simple proposition, which can also be expressed in the form of a single clause without a change in truth conditions."

(v) Huddleston and Pullum (2002, p.1417): "(Cleft sentences are) defined structurally as the formula It/ demonstrative pronoun +BE+foregrounded bit+(rel CL)."

(vi) Pavey (2003, p.1): "The cleft sentence is a marked syntactic bi-clausal option which expresses a simple semantic proposition; in terms of information structure, the construction places an element in-focus position, within a copula matrix clause."

Although Delin and Oberlander (2005) did not provid a strict definition of cleft sentences, they identified four key characteristics that encapsulate their essential properties: uniqueness, the presuppositional nature of the construction, a separateness between information structure and presupposition, and stativeness.

Most of these definitions or descriptions are syntax-oriented and apply to Indo-European languages as English. However, the syntactic partition of the sentence into a relative clause and a matrix clause is not applicable to Chinese counterparts. The focus marker "shi" and the particle "de" are only inserted elements, and they do not influence the syntactic structure of the original basic sentence[①]. So, the definitions from the syntactic perspective are not borrowed in the case of Chinese. Comparatively, the characteristics of cleft sentences proposed by Delin and Oberlander's (2005) is a cross-linguistic summary, expressing cleft sentences' semantic and functional features. The present study is an informational and functional-oriented one, so pragmatic and functional criteria of cleft sentences are applied.

Jespersen's studies can be considered the most original and classical ones. His latter studies explored cleft sentences in the field of semantics and pragmatics.

Jespersen made the following observation in 1927:

" ... (Restrictive clauses introduced by it is) are interesting from a logical point of view because it is not really the antecedent (or what looks like the antecedent) that is restricted by a relative clause. When we say 'it

---

[①] Keenan (1975) distinguished the notion of "basic sentence" by the following two criteria. (i) A sentence A is more basic than a sentence B if, and only if, the syntactic form and the meaning of B are understood as a function of that A (i.e., the form of B is some modification [possibly an addition to] that of A, and the meaning of B is some modification of that of A). (ii) A sentence is a basic sentence in L if and only if no other sentence of L is more basic than it.

is the wife that decides' or 'it was the Colonel I was looking for', what we mean is really 'the wife is the deciding person' and 'the Colonel was the man I was looking for': the relative clause thus might be said to belong rather to 'it' than to the predicative following after 'it is'." (p. 88f)

Jespersen, in his later works (1937, pp.83–89), offered a critical reassessment of his earlier account, which he termed the "transposition theory." Instead, he reinterpreted this type of relative clause as a special form of "parenthetic clause", by which he was referring to what is now known as the cleft sentence. From then on, the concept of "cleft sentence" officially emerged. The following items are the syntactic properties of cleft sentences proposed by Jespersen and summarized by Lambrecht (2001, p. 464).

(i) The relative clause and the preceding predicative phrase must be adjacent to each other.

(ii) They cannot be separated by a pause.

(iii) They are 'intonationally coherent'.

(iv) The relative pronoun or marker may be absent in some languages.

(v) In English, 'that' is used preferably to 'who' or 'which'.

(vi) In English and French, no comma is used before the relative clause.

(vii) Almost universally, the relative-clause verb agrees in person and number with the immediate antecedent.

(viii) There are languages, like Italian, where no pronoun corresponding to 'it' is used.

(ix) There is no possible substitute for 'it' when the element following 'it' is an adverb or a similar word.

(x) Unlike ordinary antecedents of relative clauses, 'it' cannot be stressed.

To replace the transposition analysis, Jespersen took the sequence "it is", together with the "connective word" (the relative pronoun or marker), as a kind of "extraposition," symbolized by "[ ]"; and he treated the rest of the sentence as if the extraposed words were absent. Thus, in the sentence, "It is the wife that (or who) decides" (cf. Lambrecht, 2001) "wife" is not a P (predicative) but an S (subject), and the words "it" and "is" are what Jespersen called the "lesser subject and verb," symbolized by lower-case s and v.

(2-1)　It is **the wife** that decides: [sv] S [3c] V[①]

(2-2)　It is **the wife** who decides: [sv] S [sc] V

A cleft sentence without a connective word, such as "It was John we saw" is represented as follow.

(2-3)　It was **John** we saw: [sv] O S V

With this representation, Jespersen observed the intuition of native speakers, which tells that the cleft sentences are semantically equivalent to the canonical noncopula sentences, so sentences (2-1), (2-2) and (2-3) are semantically equivalent to the sentences "The wife decides" and "We saw John". He also observed that the speakers' pragmatic intuition tells that (2-1) and (2-2) are related to the subject-accented "The **wife** decides", while (2-3) is related to the object-accented "focus-movement" structure **John** we saw.

Typologically, Jespersen also offered the following explanation for the use of cleft structures across languages:

"In some, though not in all cases, this construction may be considered one of the means by which the disadvantages of having a comparatively rigid grammatical word order (SVO) can be obviated. This explains why it is that similar constructions are not found, or are not used extensively, in languages in which the word order is considerably less rigid than in English, French, or Scandinavian languages, thus German, Spanish, and Slavic." (Jespersen, 1937, p.85)

Finally, Jespersen (1949) proposed the following interpretations of the functional use of cleft sentences:

"A cleaving of a sentence by means of it is (often followed by a relative pronoun or connective) serves to single out one particular element of the

---

① [3c] and [sc] stand for the connectives that and who, respectively.

sentence and, very often, by directing attention to it and bringing it, as it were, into focus, to mark a contrast." (p.147).

To sum up, Jespersen (1927; 1937; 1949) coined the name of the "cleft" sentence in English; and then defined the syntactic properties and functions of English cleft sentences. By relating functions with syntactic forms, he typologically concluded that languages with less rigid word order may use cleft sentences more seldom.

2.1.2 The classifications and syntactic structures of English cleft sentences

Like many scholars, Collins (1991a) classified English cleft sentences into three main types — *it*-clefts, basic *wh*-clefts, and reversed *wh*-clefts. Examples (2-5) (2-6) and (2-7) represent the three types deriving from the canonical sentence (2-4).

(2-4)　They were discussing pragmatics.
(2-5)　It was **pragmatics** that they were discussing.
(2-6)　What they were discussing was **pragmatics**.
(2-7)　**Pragmatics** was what they were discussing.

In addition to these three main types, cleft sentences also include several distinct subtypes. They are *if-because*-clefts, *all*-clefts, *since*-clefts, and *only*- clefts (Collins, 1991a) . However, this study does not examine these additional cleft variants, as they fall beyond its primary scope.

By observing and summarizing the phenomenon of clefts and pseudo-clefts, Collins put forward his models of the structure of the two constructions based on Prince's theoretical framework. According to Prince (1978), the structure of English cleft is: *It is/was C which/ who(m) / that S-C* (S=sentence, C=constituent). Collins (1991a, p.36) later expanded upon this structure, refining its formulation as follows (see Figure 2-1).

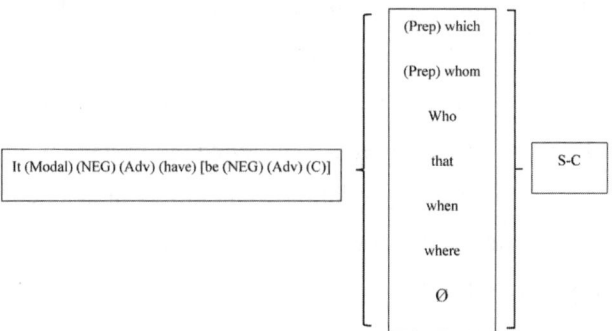

Figure 2-1 Structure of the English cleft sentence (Collins,1991a: 36)

  The structure of English cleft sentences has been the subject of extensive scholarly debate. Broadly speaking, existing studies can be categorized into two main theoretical approaches — the structural and the transformational schools — based on the distinct aspects of cleft constructions each framework emphasizes.

  Structural studies on cleft sentences mainly discuss the formal structures of cleft sentences. It was Poutsma (1928) who first observed the existence of the construction, although the term "cleft" was coined by Jespersen(1937). In his book, Poutsma held the view that the words string "it be ... that" is semantically empty and that it is merely used for structural purposes. Poutsma observed that the structure of the cleft sentence is the artificial expedient of a typical sentence to get an effect of giving prominence to "the word (group) which indicates the foremost notion in the speaker's thoughts" (Poustma,1928,p.140). The objectives of the studies of Quirk et al.(1985) are mainly concerned with the use of "it", the restrictions of the focus,the relative clause,and the information processing. Considering the use of "it",they stated that "it" is the most neutral and semantically unmarked one among the personal pronouns, and it is used as an "empty" or "prop" subject, especially in expressions denoting time, distance or atmospheric conditions (1985, p. 348). Furthermore, it is important to highlight the significant contributions of Quirk et al. to the study of restrictions on focus in cleft constructions.

According to their analysis, subjects, direct objects, and adjuncts can freely occupy the focus position, whereas indirect objects and object complements can only marginally serve as the initial focus in cleft sentences. More commonly, an indirect object is replaced by a prepositional phrase in this syntactic structure. Additionally, the use of subject complements as focus elements is subject to strict constraints, particularly when the verb "be" appears at the end of the second clause and when the subject complement is realized as an adjectival phrase.

Transformational analyses of cleft sentences primarily investigate their underlying or deep structure, with a particular emphasis on their syntactic origins. Scholars in this field have proposed at least four distinct explanations regarding the derivation of cleft constructions.

Lees (1963) is one of the earliest scholars who analyzed cleft sentences from a transformational-generative point of view. He believed that the cleft sentence is a modification of its corresponding simple sentence. A cleft can be changed from a simple sentence by bringing the selected pivotal expression to the front of the sentence. He also proposed that the cleft sentences may be followed by a prefixed WH-morpheme generated by the derivation of the pivotal expression (p.377). Akmajian (1970) claimed that "the cleft sentence is syntactically derived from the pseudo-cleft sentence with the rule of 'extraposition', by which the initial clause of the pseudo-cleft sentence is moved from the end of the sentence" (p.149). The third version of the source of clefts is given by Gundel (1988). She also assumed that the cleft sentence is derived from the pseudo-cleft, but the derivation method is "right-dislocation". Considering the two classifications of pseudo-cleft sentences, Gundel claimed that only identificational equative pseudo-clefts can generate clefts, while attributive pseudo-clefts cannot. Delahunty (1984) and Knowles (1986) drew a similar conclusion that cleft sentence is universally "base-generated" regardless of the language differences (Knowles, 1986, pp. 295–317), and the cleft sentence, pseudo-cleft, and their corresponding simple sentences are synonymous at the level of logical structure, so it is inappropriate to say that any of them is derived from the others.

Since Chinese cleft sentences do not involve syntactic movement from an underlying base structure, the transformational approach is generally considered inapplicable to their analysis.

2.1.3　Semantic features of English cleft sentences

Semantically, certain characteristics of cleft sentences have been widely agreed by scholars (Hole, 2011; Huang, 2010; Kiss, 1998). The key semantic properties are outlined as follows.

2.1.3.1 Dichotomization of meaning

As Huang (2010, p.14) asserted, " a cleft sentence has the universal semantic property of dichotomizing a sentence into focus and presupposition … ". The structural distribution of the cleft sentences mainly consists of "presupposition" and "focus", though the terminology may vary across different studies.

In his analysis, Collins (1991a) examined the relationship between these two contrasting constituents, emphasizing the identifying function of cleft sentences rather than their attributive role. He argued that cleft sentences function as identifying constructions, establishing a relationship of identity between the highlighted element and the relative clause.

A critical distinction to consider is that, as identifying constructions, clefts and pseudo-clefts must be differentiated from other superficially similar attributive sentences. Collins further clarified this distinction by analyzing the fundamental nature of identifying sentences and attributive sentences, outlining their key differences.

Attributive construction expresses a relationship between an entity and some attribute that is ascribed to it, be it an indication of class membership, a quality, role or other such characteristic; identification is a relationship between two entities, characteristic, the one serving to define the identity of the other. While identifying constructions are typically reversible, attributive constructions are not. (Collins, 1991a, p.15)

Hole (2011) proposed his criteria and features of cleft sentences as the follows.

(i) Partition — there is a syntactic partition between the cleft constituent and an open sentence (i.e. presupposition).

(ii) Cleft focus — the cleft constituent often contains focal material.

(iii) Cleft presupposition — the open sentence is presupposed.

(iv) Clefts are never necessarily additive — in the absence of contradicting material, the cleft focus is never restricted to an additive reading.

(v) Topic/ frame-setter — cleft sentences may depend on overt topic or frame-setters. (p. 1709)

These five properties delineate the interaction between presupposition, focus, and topic, shedding light on the structural and functional relationships within cleft constructions.

2.1.3.2 Exhaustivity of the focus constituent

Kiss (1998) proposed two semantic properties of cleft sentences — exhaustiveness and exclusiveness. The first property describes that the constituent under contrastive focus in a sentence is a complete list of the entities that make the truth value of the proposition true. The second property says that those and only those entities under contrastive focus will make the truth value of the proposition true, excluding other entities (Li, 2008, p.760).

Büring and Kriz (2013) defined the "exhaustivity claim" as:

"A cleft of the form *It is x that p* not only expresses that x has property p, but also that x is the only individual to have p, i.e., that x exhaustively identifies p (in the relevant contextual domain)." (p.1)

To explain these properties, English example (2-8) is provided.

(2-8) It was **pragmatics** that they were discussing.

In the above sentence, the set "They were discussing X" with "X" representing the variables suitable for the expression of the set "What they are discussing". The set may be {pragmatics, semantics, syntax, math, etc.}. To assign the variable "pragmatics" to "X" makes the proposition a completed one, which is called "assertion", and the focused constituent "pragmatics" is an exhaustive focus.

Delin and Oberlander (2005) expressed this similar property of cleft sentences with a different term . In their study, cleft sentences convey "uniqueness", which determines that the set of the cleft constituents is an exhaustive listing of the elements presupposed by the cleft clause.

A central debate concerning the exhaustivity of cleft sentences revolves around its origins, specifically the source of the exhaustive effect. Two competing explanations have been proposed. The semantic origin hypothesis argues that exhaustivity is inherently encoded in the meaning of cleft sentences, functioning either as a presupposition (Percus, 1997; Hedberg, 2000; Hedberg and Fadden, 2007; Hedberg, 2013) or as a conventional implicature (Halvorsen, 1977; Collins, 1991a). In contrast, the pragmatic origin hypothesis contends that exhaustivity is not an intrinsic semantic property but rather a result of conversational/conventional implicature, as suggested by studies such as Horn (1981) for English, Dufter (2009) for English, German, and several Romance languages (including Italian), and Roggia (2009) for Italian. This ongoing discussion continues to explore whether exhaustivity is a semantically encoded feature or a pragmatic inference derived from discourse context.

2.1.4 Functions of English cleft sentences

Regarding the discourse perspective, the functions of cleft sentences are widely discussed by scholars, and they reached the consensus that the primary function of cleft sentences is the function of focusing (Chomsky, 1972; Lambrecht, 2001; Prince, 1978).

Besides, scholars (e.g., Collins, 2002; Li, 2008) agreed on the contrastive emphasis of cleft sentences by the particular syntactic layout derived from a canonical sentence. To quote from Collins (2002):

"The key to why they have evolved as a resource in the English language, I shall assume, is a consideration of a speaker's communicative needs — the need to select, at a given point in a discourse, a form that is appropriate in the light of assumptions about what information an addressee already possesses, the need to select a form which appropriately emphasizes or focuses upon particular parts of the message, the need to draw a particular contrast, and so forth." (p. 4)

However, two issues should be taken into consideration.

Firstly, contrastivity is not the particular function possessed only by cleft sentences. In any language, be it English, Chinese, or other languages, there are other ways to realize the function of contrastive emphasis morphologically, syntactically, or pragmatically. To name a few, the English "even" sentences; the object-preposing in both English and Chinese; the usage of accent in English, and the change of tone in Chinese are all methods of expressing contrastive emphasis. The differences between other syntactic structures and cleft sentences will be explained as the distinguishing properties (and criteria) of cleft sentences later. Scholars have also suggested that the discourse function of the "it-cleft" is inherently contrastive (cf. Hedberg, 1988; Biber et al., 1999) and plays a crucial role in "unambiguous marking of the focus of information in written English, where the cue of intonation is absent" (cf. Quirk et al., 1985, p.951). It is being "oriented towards newness" that leads to a "higher communicative dynamism" (Collins, 1991b, p. 514) than in other cleft types. Aside from this more general function, the "it-cleft" can be used for "expressing a connection to a preceding text" (Biber et al., 1999, p. 962) and also as a "remind me" toll (Miller, 1996).

Secondly, cleft sentences serve functions beyond contrastivity. Scholars examining cleft constructions in languages other than English emphasize the diverse communicative roles these structures fulfill. For example, Garassino

(2016) classified Italian cleft sentences into new-focus, contrastive, and non-contrastive cleft sentences. New-focus cleft sentences refer to those in which the focal constituent does not show contrast, the set of focus substitutions is not finite, and the focal substitution is an unidentifiable referent. Contrastive cleft sentences refer to those in which the focal component is decoded in an explicit (i.e, as a response to a choice interrogative) or implicit manner (i.e., the set of focus substitutions can be built by relying on semantic inference) by the listener/reader in this discourse. Garassino (2016) identified two principal functions in Italian cleft sentences expressing non-contrastive focus: cohesive textual and performative functions. Through his investigation, more than half of the Italian cleft sentences express a non-contrastive function, while in the English corpus, more than half of the cleft sentences express a contrastive function, so there are significant differences between English and Italian cleft sentences considering different functions. Similarly, Cassarà et al. (2022) found that French cleft sentences encode both contrastive focus and informational focus functions. Their corpus analysis revealed that a significantly greater proportion of cleft constructions serve an informational focus function rather than a contrastive focus function.

2.2 Cross-linguistic Perspectives on Cleft Sentences

For studies of cleft sentences in non-English languages, especially in European languages, the method of *translation* is applied (Delin and Oberlander, 2005). This approach takes a cleft in the context of a source language, examines its translation and thus makes a contrastive study from the comparison. The translation approach is widely practised in European and particularly Scandinavian studies (see Aijmer et.al, 1996).

This section introduces the literature on cleft sentences in French,

Italian, German, and Japanese. Some contrastive studies are conducted to compare the acceptability of cleft sentences in different languages. It is widely accepted that clefts are a diagnostic feature of neo-standard Italian, a contemporary variety of Italian (Berruto, 1987; Sabatini, 1985). Furthermore, recent research indicates a growing frequency in the use of cleft sentences in Italian. In French, cleft sentences are considered a standard and integral linguistic structure, frequently occuring as a "vital construction found with great frequency in spoken and written French" (Katz, 2000, p. 253). By contrast, their usage is more restricted in German, where clefts are confined to specific registers (Altmann, 2009), and in English, where they are primarily associated with formal and higher speech registers (Collins, 1991a, p. 185).

De Cesare et al. (2014) conducted a contrastive analysis examining the form and frequency of cleft sentences across different languages using corpus data. Their findings suggested that canonical cleft constructions — such as it-clefts in English and their equivalents in other languages — are generally reported to occur with greater frequency in French than in most other major Romance languages (Dufter, 2008) as well as in English (Katz, 2000).

Miller (2006) proposed his typological differences in cleft sentences in English, German, and French as:

"English is the most striking in having three cleft sentences, which are not only described in the grammar of English but are in frequent use and occur in the English map task dialogues (and, of course, in conversation and writing). Other Indo-European languages have one cleft sentence or two, but not three. French has IT-cleft and WH-cleft [… but no Reverse WH-cleft]. German has clefts, which occur far less frequently than in English, but it has frequently-occurring particles." (pp. 203-204)

The following sections present a review of previous research on cleft constructions in French, Italian, German, and Japanese, highlighting cross-linguistic similarities and differences.

2.2.1　Cleft Sentences in French

In French, the "c'est cleft" is used to mark the focus. As previously noted, languages employ a variety of strategies for making focus, utilizing different structural and prosodic mechanisms. English, for example, relies heavily on prosody to mark focus, while French makes comparatively greater use of syntactic constructions to communicate the same focus relations (Katz, 2000; Lambrecht, 2010). In French, the "c'est cleft" is a widely-used method to express focus, as exemplified in (2-9).

(2-9)　C'est **Madeleine** qui chantait dans le couloir.
　　　It is Madeleine REL sing-IMP. 33G in the hall.
　　　It's **Madeleine** who was singing in the hall.

Lambrecht (1994) claimed that using the "c'est" cleft is to be pragmatically motivated to mark focus on elements that occur in positions where French disallows prosodic marking (i.e., French categorically bans prosodic marking from the sentence-initial position). So, he concluded that "c'est-clefts" are used to mark focus on arguments, in other words, by the focus types[①] proposed by Lambrecht himself, the focus type of "c'est-clefts" can only be the argument focus.

Subsequent studies provided different opinions on the structure of cleft sentences. Belletti (2005) analyzed clefts as a single CP and Lambrecht (1994) categorized them as a construction, Clech-Darbon et al. (1999) challenged the notion that French possesses true cleft sentences in the traditional sense. Instead, they proposed that clefts should be interpreted as a combination of an identificational TP, where the focused constituent functions as a complement, and an adjoining CP positioned to the right. In this framework, the CP operates as a standard relative clause, with a relative operator moving

---

[①] Departing from the focusing function of structures, Lambrecht (1994) divided the types of focus structures into three criteria according to the syntactic classes of the focused constituents—predicate-focus structure, argument-focus structure, and sentence-focus structure.

from SpecTP to SpecCP.

Hamlaoui (2008) agreed with this idea. She proposed that there is one advantage of analyzing the cleft in this way, namely that it makes correct predictions regarding prosody: main stress falls on the rightmost edge of an intonational phrase in French, and by creating two separate IPs, the cleft allows the focus element to receive main stress and to fulfill the rightmost preference of the language for accent placement. She also argued that a cleft sentence is preferred over a canonical sentence under two circumstances: to answer the subject-constituent questions and to present contrastive/corrective contexts. Her study challenged Lambrecht's in that she postulated no need for the focused constituent or the main stress to move a dedicated focus position. Instead, she argued that the mapping of phonology and syntax allows the focused constituent to be directly merged in the position where grammar assigns the main stress (rightmost). Grammatical subjects are realized in a cleft to receive the rightmost stress when focused, and grammatical objects remain in situ.

Belletti (2005) argued that when responding to a subject-related question, cleft constructions are generally more acceptable due to their prominent role in marking subject focus. However, in cases where the question pertains to the object, cleft sentences are less preferred, as they are considered computationally costly. Instead, in-situ parallelism is favored as a more efficient and economical response strategy.

With regard to the semantic and formal analysis of French cleft constructions, only a limited number of studies have examined them from the perspective of exhaustivity. Representative works include Clech-Darbon et al. (1999) and Doetjes et al. (2004), among others. Clech-Darbon et al. (1999) examined the truth-conditional exhaustivity of cleft constructions and argued that the focus constituent falls within the scope of an exhaustive operator. Doetjes et al. (2004), on the other hand, proposed that exhaustivity in cleft sentences arises specifically when the focused element is referential. The exhaustivity is also studied as one of the discourse functions of "c'est" cleft by Lambrecht (1994), Katz (1997), and deCat (2007). They all expressed the exhaustivity in the way of "identifying the X as having the property P, carrying the inference that nothing else in the context displays the property P" (Destruel, 2012, p. 98).

In summary, existing research on French cleft sentences has primarily focused on their syntactic structure, with particular attention given to the eligibility and necessity of cleft constructions in French. Additionally, the notion of exhaustivity has sparked ongoing debates regarding whether it should be considered a core function or an inherent semantic property of French cleft sentences.

2.2.2 Cleft Sentences in Italian

The widely-accepted form of the cleft sentence in Italian is a null subject sentence, shown in example (2-10).

(2-10) a. Chi è partito/haparlato? (Quoted from Belletti, 2005)
Who be. 3SG leave. PST. PTCP/have. 3SG speak. PST. PTCP?
Who has left/spoken?
b.È partito/haparlato **Gianni**.
be. 3SG leave. PST. PTCP/ have. 3SG speak. PST. PTCP Gianni.
has left/has spoken Gianni.
Gianni has left/spoken.

Belletti (2005) illustrated:

"In a null subject language like Italian, a sentence containing a postverbal subject, focus on new information should correspond to a representation along the line as:

[CP ... [TP pro ... e ... partito/ ha parlato ... [TopP [FocP Gianni [TopP [VP ...]]]]]]" (p. 3)

Beninca (1978), Frison (1982, 2001), Graffi (1978), and Grewendorf and Poletto (1989) explored cleft sentences in Italian from a generative perspective; and cleft sentences have been investigated diachronically by Metzeltin (1989) and Sornicola (1991). Cleft sentences in unique variants or genres have also been studied by De Stefani (2009) from a functional perspective.

Despite the extensive studies, a fundamental question remains unsolved: whether these constructions are inherently characteristic of Italian, widely accepted by native speakers, or fully integrated into the languages grammatical system.

Belletti (2005) declared that, for reasons of economy, inversion derivation is directly available in a null subject language like Italian, so it is adopted as it involves less structure and, consequently, less computation, than a cleft. However, the structure of the cleft sentence is not denied by any grammatical reason, and in fact, cleft sentences seem natural if they are prompted by questions.

"All other things being equal, null subject languages, as standard Italian, can exploit the inversion strategy marking the use of the dedicated focus position in the VP periphery, with a silent preverbal subject. In languages where the null subject parameter is set negatively, one of two strategies appears to be utilized to realize new information subject: i. creating a non-null subject compatible 'inversion ' structure, exploiting the informational content of the VP periphery; ii. adopting a (DP internal) focus-in-situ strategy. French and English illustrate the two options. The quite typical cleft answer, widely adopted in French, has been interpreted here as a kind of 'inversion in disguise ' sharing important properties with subject inversion/ VS structures of Italian type." (Belletti, 2005, p.18).

From the perspective of informational structure, alternative syntactic strategies have been identified for encoding focus within a sentence. Besides subject-verb inversion and cleft formation, Italian also offers focus fronting. Although such structures as 'focus fronting ' and cleft sentences realize a similar function, they are not equivalent. For cleft sentences, exhaustive interpretation is embedded; however, there is no exhaustive interpretation in focus fronting constructions (cf. Brunetti, 2004; Delin and Oberlander, 2005; Frascarelli and Ramaglia, 2013). Obviously, exhaustivity is also considered a property and a criterion of cleft sentences in Italian.

Taking cleft sentences as a legitimate existence of Italian, contrastive studies are conducted by some scholars. From a typological point of view, Lambrecht (1994) pointed out that cleft formation is a possible alternative in English and Italian but is obligatory in French; while for German, he claimed that cleft formation is a highly unnatural construction used in some given context.

In summary, scholarly debate persists regarding issues such as the authenticity and status of cleft sentences in Italian.

Nevertheless, scholars have reached a general consensus that the classifications of cleft constructions established within the framework of English do not adequately account for their counterparts in Romance languages, particularly Italian. First of all, the label IT-cleft is not suitable for pro-drop languages such as Italian because, in these languages, sentences are not started with any form of pronoun. Secondly, the label WH-cleft is also problematic since in Romance languages, it is also supposed to refer to sentences that are not started with a wh-word (i.e., by a free relative pronoun of the form "chi/qui/quien (who)" or "dove/ou/donde (where)" in Italian, French and Spanish, respectively) but by a complex pronoun, such as "Quello che" in Italian, "Ce que" in French, "Lo que" in Spanish, all representing "what" (De Cesare et al., 2014). Thirdly, exhaustivity is the semantic property of cleft sentences in both French and Italian.

2.2.3 Cleft Sentences in German

Although certain syntactic issues concerning German cleft constructions remain unresolved, Fischer (2009) proposed the structure "es/it + form of sein/be + X [stressed] + subordinate (relative) clause" as the prototypical form, commonly known in German as "the Spaltsatz". For example:

(2-11)   Es ist **Plato**, der unseres Wissens als erster explizit zwischen Nomina und Verben unterscheidet.
EXPL COP Plato REL our.GEN knowledge. GEN as first explicitly between nouns and verbs distinguish.3SG.
It is **Plato**, who, to our knowledge, first explicitly distinguishes between Nouns and Verbs.

As previously noted, the syntactic issues addressed in the preceding sections primarily concern the legitimacy of cleft constructions in German, particularly in relation to the constraints imposed by the language's information-structural properties.

Durrell (2002, p. 479) observed that unlike German, which can easily move clause elements into the initial position to form the sentence's topic, English requires a range of complex sentences corresponding to simple sentences in German. Although German and English cleft have similar syntactic configurations, their stylistic value and information structure are very different. The following items are the basic facts of German cleft sentences (Durrell, 2002).

(i) Cleft constructions occur significantly less frequently in German than in English.

(ii) This disparity can be attributed to the differing fronting mechanisms available in the two languages.

(iii) In German, cleft sentences often sound unnatural.

(iv) A more natural interpretation of cleft constructions in German is often realized as an extension of an alternative syntactic structure.

Prior to Durrell (2002), Doherty (1999, p. 293) observed that "there are hardly any studies of German clefts alone" and noted that "even German linguists seem to find the English side more rewarding" . Ahlemeyer and Kohlhof (1999) conducted a corpus-based study examining the translation of English cleft sentences into German. Their findings indicated that only approximately one-third of English it-cleft constructions are rendered as direct German equivalents. Instead, monoclausal structures that emphasize a focused XP are more commonly employed to fulfill the same functional role as cleft sentences in German. Even earlier, Engel (1988) "warned" learners of German not to overuse clefts, although he considers subject clefting, case complement clefting, and prepositional complement clefts grammatically acceptable.

Focusing on translation studies and addressing the discrepancy in the frequency of cleft constructions between English and German, Fischer (2009) argued that, beyond structural differences, incorporating stylistic factors provides a more precise explanation. English, as a more verb-oriented language, tends to favor subordinate clause constructions over non-clausal alternatives. In several respects, English verbal constructions exhibit greater semantic explicitness compared to their German non-clausal counterparts (Fischer, 2009, pp.392-398).

In conclusion, although cleft constructions are recognized in German grammatical descriptions (see Zifonun et al., 1997, among others), the dominant scholarly view remains cautious, often questioning their naturalness and marked preference within the syntactic repertoire of German.

2.2.4　Cleft Sentences in Japanese

According to Hasegawa (1997), the cleft sentence is characterized by the structure [... *no wa/ga*} X *da*]. Particles "*wa*" and "*ga*" construct the Japanese cleft sentence.

(2-12)　John-ga kinoo eki de atta no-wa Mary da.
　　　　John-NOM yesterday station LOC meet. PST NMLZ-TOP Mary COP.

It was **Mary** who John met at the station yesterday.

(2-13) John-ga kinoo eki de atta no-ga Mary da.

John-NOM yesterday station LOC meet-PST NMLZ-NOM Mary COP.

The person whom John met at the station yesterday was Mary.

Kuno (1973) proposed that the pronominal form "no" can be marked with either the topic particle "wa" or the nominative particle "ga". The two types correspond relatively to cleft and pseudo-cleft sentences in English from the translation perspective. The particles "wa" and "ga" make a crucial difference in the focus interpretation between the two clefts. In the "wa-cleft", the focus is on the noun phrase "Mary" in the predicate; while in the "ga-cleft", the focus is on the clause "John ga kinoo eki de atta no" in the subject position, which is a preposed focus structure (see Sunakawa, 1995).

Similar to their English counterparts, Japanese counterparts have been widely discussed from the perspective of generative grammar (see Hasegawa, 1997; Hiraiwa and Ishihara, 2002; Hoji, 1987; Kizu, 2005; Koizumi, 1995; Takahashi, 2006; Hoji and Ueyama, 1998 among others). There are two different results on the generative syntactic structure of cleft sentences in Japanese. The first explains that the focus phrase is base-generated in its surface position with an operator movement inside the presuppositional clause, which is very similar to the analysis of the (it-) cleft in English. The other involves the movement of the focus phrase and the subsequent remnant movement of the presuppositional clause.

Following the terminology in Hoji (1987), cleft sentences in Japanese are divided into two types. The sentences with the case marker on the focus NP are CM[①]-cleft, and those without the case marker are Non-CM-cleft. I present an example of each type, as cited from Hoji and Ueyama (1998).

---

① CM stands for "case marker".

2.2.4.1 CM-Cleft

(2-14) [Kokuren-ga / kibisiku/ [so-re-o] ₁/ hihansita/ no]-wa/ [**amerika-no/booei-seisaku-o**]₁ /da.①
The United Nations-NOM / harshly/ that-thing-ACC/criticized/ COMP-TOP/ USA-GEN/ defense-policy-ACC/ be.
It was [**the USA 's defense policy-ACC**]₁ that the United Nations harshly criticized it₁.

2.2.4.2 Non-CM-CLEFT

(2-15) [Syuukansi-ga/ [neta-ni/ tumaru/ to] /yoku /[so-re-o]₁/ tokusyuusuru/no]-wa/ [daietto /to /onsen]₁/ da.
Magazine-NOM/ topic-DAT/ stuck/ if/ often/ that-thing-ACC/ feature/ COMP-TOP/ **diet/ and/ spa/ be**.
It is [**diet and hot spa**]₁ that magazines often feature [it/them]₁ [when they are stuck for topics].

Based on observation, they claim an empty operator movement in the CM-cleft sentences, but there is no movement in Non-CM-cleft sentences.

Kizu (2005) analyzed the cleft sentence in Japanese from its topicalization, nominalization, dependency, and ellipsis. He proposed that there does exist operator movement in Japanese cleft sentences. However, the question of "how the movement takes place" differs dramatically.

"In English, it is generally assumed that the null operator moves successive-cyclically; however, this is different from what we have found to hold in Japanese. Instead, the null operator of Japanese long-distance clefts is base-generated adjoined to the highest embedded clause in the presuppositional clause and undergoes short movement to the spec of CP. Short A'-movement is also observed in local clefts; the operator first

---

① The numbered footnote "1" shows the co-referential relationship.

undergoes A-movement to sentence-initial position, and then further A'-movement takes place." (Kizu, 2005, pp. 205-206)

2.3 Summary

The term "cleft sentences" originated in English, leading to a more extensive and well-established body of research on English cleft constructions. In contrast, studies on cleft sentences in other languages have primarily centered on their grammaticality and acceptability within their respective linguistic systems. As noted, whether cleft constructions serve as the preferred means of expressing the same functional distinctions as their English counterparts remains a subject of debate in the analysis of French, Italian, and German cleft sentences. In contrast, research on Japanese cleft constructions generally acknowledges them as a natural strategy for marking focus and contrastive emphasis. In summary, there is a strong scholarly advocacy for establishing universal evaluative criteria to define and analyze cleft constructions across languages.

Chapter 3

Cleft Sentences in Chinese

To date, scholars have widely acknowledged the long-established tradition of identifying "shi (NP/PP/AdvP) ... (VP) de" as the Chinese cleft sentence. (Teng, 1979; Fang, 1995; Huang and Fawcett, 1996; Shang, 2002; Paul and Whitman, 2008). However, they also recognized that this "shi (NP/ PP/ AdvP) ... (VP) de" structure-hereafter referred to as "shi ... de" clefts-exhibits significant structural and functional differences from its English counterpart, namely the "it is ... that" construction.

Paul and Whitman (2008) proposed that the distinguishing syntactic property of " shi ... de" clefts is that they involve no A'movement. This fact is because the presupposition in the " shi ... de " clefts involves a projection smaller than CP. Chinese "shi ... de" clefts lack a landing site for A'movement and fail to host material such as negation, usually compatible with full CP clefts in languages such as English. The difference can be traced back to the semantic/pragmatic prominence phenomenon in Chinese (Huang, 1982, 1988, 2007; LaPolla, 1995; Li and Thompson, 1981), therefore the function of cleft sentences is not revealed by syntactic form, but by cleaving the proposition into two parts from the perspective of information structure.

Teng (1979) first explained the process of "cleaving" in general; and then gave the criteria of identifying Chinese cleft sentences. For him, "cleaving" is a syntactic description for marking a constituent of a sentence for focus, contrast, or emphasis by syntactic devices. Although focus, contrast or emphasis can also be indicated phonologically, cleft sentences realize the function of emphasis/ contrast by syntactically putting a specific constituent in a prominent position.

According to the general features of cleft sentences, Teng (1979) proposed that there should be three criteria for identifying Chinese cleft sentences.

(i) The presence of a syntactic marker (i.e., "shi") to single out the focused constituent.

(ii) The absence in the main clause of an NP which is co-referent to the focused constituent.

(iii) The focused constituent is consistently associated with asserted information, while the remainder of the sentence conveys presupposed content.

Two examples are quoted from his study.

(3-1)　我是**明天**要到纽约去。
　　　　Wǒ shì míngtiān yào dào Niǔyuē qù。
　　　　1SG SHI$_{aux}$ tomorrow MOD to New York go.
　　　　It is **tomorrow** that I will go to New York.

(3-2)　我是**昨天**到纽约去的。
　　　　Wǒ shì zuótiān dào Niǔyuē qù de
　　　　1SG SHI$_{aux}$ **yesterday** to New York go DE$_{ptcl}$.
　　　　It was yesterday that I went to New York.

Both sentences are recognized as cleft constructions. However, "de" functions as an optional particle, whose presence is determined by the overall structural characteristics of the sentence.

However, two problems still need to be solved in Teng's study. Firstly, he did not give any analysis of the absence or presence of "de". In other words, he did not solve the problem of under which condition "de" can be legally deleted without altering the sentence's meaning and function. Sometimes, the object and "de" can switch their positions in the sentence, but only under certain conditions (i.e., the action indicated by the embedded sentence must be in the past time, and its VP must contain an adverbial).

Secondly, he disregarded the differences between the cleft sentences he claimed and other "shi" sentences.

3.1 Forms of Chinese Cleft Sentences

Early Chinese researchers (Lü, 1944; Song, 1978; Wang, 1944) noticed a "shi … de" construction existing in Chinese aiming to express emphasis. The consensus on this language phenomenon is that there is a basic sentence beneath the cleft sentence. Moreover, the basic proposition is cleaved by "shi".

(3-3)　Basic form:

他昨天到了。

Tā zuótiān dào le.

3SG yesterday arrive LE$_{aspc}$.

He **arrived here yesterday**.

(3-4)　Cleft sentence:

他是昨天到的。

Tā shì zuótiān dào de.

3SG SHI$_{aux}$ yesterday arrive DEptcl.

It was **yesterday** that he arrived.

(3-5)　Basic form:

他第一个写完作业。

Tā dì-yī gè xiěwán zuòyè.

3SG first write-finish homework.

He **was the first person who finished his homework**.

(3-6)　Cleft sentence:

是他第一个写完作业的。

Shì tā dì-yī gè xiěwán zuòyè de.

SHI$_{aux}$ 3SG first-finish-CL write-PFV homework DE$_{ptcl}$.

It was **him** who finished the homework first.

Sentences (3-4) and (3-6) are both cleft sentences; however, (3-4) puts focus on the adjunct of the sentence (being the following constituent of the focus marker "shi"),while sentence (3-6) puts focus on the subject of the sentence.

To interpret the aforementioned Chinese cleft sentences, Zhao (1979) argued that in the sentence "shi … de", "shi" is not the primary verb; instead, it is placed before the verb or the adjunct to denote the emphasis; "de" is placed behind the verb, indicating the tense/aspectual feature of the primary verb, typically indicating that the action or situation has been completed or realized. Liu (1983) assumed that what fills the gap between " shi" and "de" is mainly the verb, verb phrases or the subject-predicate phrases with the verb as the predicate. The focus of the cleft sentence is not the action itself but aspects related to the action, such as time, place, manner, condition, purpose, object or agent.

Other scholars (e.g., Hashimoto, 1969; Tang, 1983; Zhang and Fang, 1996) related the Chinese "shi … de" sentence to the English cleft sentence. Tang (1983) considered the Chinese cleft as a construction with a judgment verb "shi" and particle "de" expressing assertion while separating the whole sentence into two: the first part as the presupposition and the second part as the focus. Zhang and Fang (1996) held that "shi … de" is the focus-marking sentence in Chinese, and "shi" is the focus marker followed by the emphatic part.

3.2 Classifications of Chinese "shi⋯de" Sentences

Paul and Whitman (2008) proposed several forms of cleft sentences derived from "shi … de". They subcategorized the classifications of cleft sentences into cleft focus patterns, represented by the sentence-initial bare "shi" (subject focus only) and the "shi … de" proper (subject and adjunct focus); association with focus pattern, represented by the sentence-medial bare "shi"; and the propositional assertion which involves the copula "shi" and a marker of clausal subordination.

Paul and Whitman (2008) analyzed "shi … de" and bare "shi" as two distinct constructions with entirely different properties. They considered constructions with bare "shi" associated with focus constructions instead of cleft sentences. According to them, the distinctions are as follows:

"(... the shi ... de) construction shows a bipartitioning consisting of the focused element and the presupposition, which is always outside the scope of negation; it is subject to the exclusiveness condition, and focus is positionally determined. In the bare shi construction, by contrast, any constituent to the right of "shi" that is marked by intonational prominence may be associated with focus, and the exclusiveness condition does not hold." (p. 420)

To explain the difference, Paul and Whitman (2008) refined the classifications of cleft sentences into the cleft focus pattern, including "sentence-initial bare shi" construction and "shi ... de proper" constructions; the association with focus pattern that refers to medial "shi" sentences, and propositional assertions. To illustrate by several examples.

(3-7)　是我负责这件事。
　　　　Shì wǒ fùzé zhè jiàn shì.
　　　　SHI_{aux} 1SG be. responsible this CL matter.
　　　　It is **I** who am responsible for this matter.

This sentence is a "sentence-initial bare shi", putting the subject as the focus.

(3-8)　我是昨天到北京的。
　　　　Wǒ shì zuótiān dào Běijīng de.
　　　　1SG SHI_{aux} yesterday arrive Beijing DE_{ptcl}.
　　　　It is **yesterday** that I arrived in Beijing.

(3-9)　是我负责这件事的。
　　　　Shì wǒ fùzé zhè jiàn shì de.
　　　　SHI_{aux} 1SG be. responsible this CL matter DE_{ptcl}.
　　　　It is **I** who am responsible for this matter.

Sentence (3-7) represents a proper "shi ... de" cleft construction, where the focus falls on the adjunct of the sentence. In contrast, sentence (3-8) exhibits a structurally similar pattern, but the focus is placed on the subject or argument instead.

The structure "sentence-medial shi" is not considered a cleft sentence by Paul and Whitman (2008). For them, any constituent in any position in the clause to the right of "shi" can be focused by prosodic prominence.

(3-10)　老魏是明天去北京。
　　　　 Lǎo Wèi shì míngtiān qù Běijīng.
　　　　 PN SHI$_{aux}$ tomorrow go Beijing.

The appropriate translation will depend on the actual intonational focus in sentence (3-10) and may correspond to one of the following options.

(3-11)　It is **tomorrow** that Laowei is going to Beijing.

　　　　 It is **Laowei** who is going (to somewhere).

　　　　 Laowei is going to **Beijing** tomorrow, not Shanghai.

(3-12)　他是跟你开玩笑的。
　　　　 Tā shì gēn nǐ kāi wánxiào de.
　　　　 3SG SHI$_{aux}$ with 2SG joke DE$_{ptcl}$.
　　　　 (It is the case that) he **was joking with you**.

Example (3-12), drawn from Chao (1968, p. 296), is identified by the author as an instance of the "propositional assertion pattern". The sentence conveys the speaker's certainty that the proposition holds in a given situation. In this structure, no specific constituent is focused, despite the presence of both "shi" and "de", as seen in the example.

Li's (2008) study categorized Chinese cleft sentences as the contrastive focus structure while classifying them into two types-one is marked by "shi", and the other by "shi...de" . So Li's study compromised Teng's (1979) and Hasimoto's (1969) ideas. Tang (1983) subdivided Chinese cleft sentences into the names "cleft sentences" , "the derivation of cleft sentences" and "pseudo-cleft sentences". His classifications are similar to those of Collins'

(1991a). One more thing worth mentioning in Teng's study is that he noticed that there is one derivational version of the Chinese cleft sentence — represented as "shi...de OBJ" with an objective following "de".

In summary, the structural configuration of Chinese cleft sentences has remained a topic of sustained academic debate, with no definitive consensus having been established to date. Current scholarly discussions primarily focus on the following two core aspects.

Ⅰ. "shi … de" vs. bare "shi" and the classifications of cleft sentences

Scholars such as Teng (1979), Huang (1982, 1988), and Chiu et al. (1993) did not give a distinguishing difference between "shi … de" and "bare shi" and proposed the same analysis for both. They mainly regarded the two constructions as possessing similar functions, and "bare shi" is just the brief version of "shi...de" with "de" omitted for the tense reason.

Zhan and Traugott (2019) subcategorized Chinese cleft sentences as cleft copula sentences showing the basic features of Chinese copula sentences. The following diagram (Figure 3-1) shows the classification of Chinese copula sentences categorized by Zhan and Traugott (2019) from the perspective of the diachronic development of Chinese. Under their categorization, Chinese cleft sentences are treated as a type of copula sentences holding semantic features as [+specificational] and [+contrastive].[1]

Ⅱ. "shi...(de)" cleft sentences vs. other "shi" sentences

Due to the inclusion of the focus marker "shi", Chinese cleft sentences are often regarded as one type of "shi" copula sentences. This study appeals a clearer division between Chinese cleft sentences and copula sentences.

Traditionally, the following four semantic categories of "shi" copula sentences in Chinese have been widely recognized and accepted.

---

[1] This present study holds a different opinion from Zhan and Traugott (2019) on the following two aspects. Firstly, Chinese cleft sentences are not regarded as copula sentences. The detailed reasons for this stance are elaborated upon in the subsequent sections. Secondly, contrastivity is not the sole function fulfilled by Chinese cleft sentences. Additional functions include topical and informative functions.

Chapter 3 Cleft Sentences in Chinese

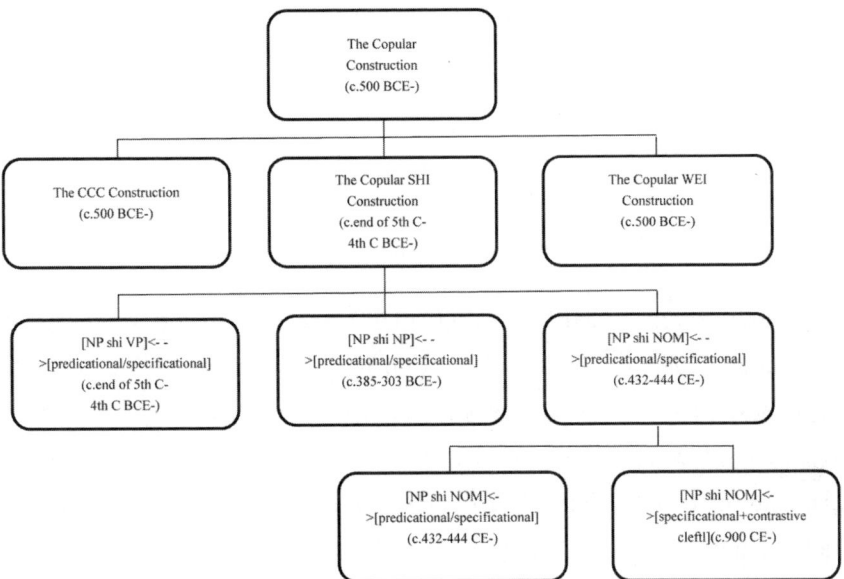

Figure 3-1 The development of the copula "shi" construction (Zhan and Traugott, 2019, P169)

(i)Equational sentences, which establish identifications, classification, etc. of entities in the sentence (e.g., 我是老师 /I am a teacher).

(ii)Attributive sentences, which describe or explain the attribution of the entities or events (e.g., 花是红的, 草是绿的 /The flower is red, and the grass is green).

(iii)Existential sentences, which indicate the existence or presence of entities in a given location (e.g., 楼下是一群小孩 /There is a group of kids downstairs).

(iv)Emphatic sentences, which serve to emphasize a specific part or the entirety of a sentence. The distinction between cleft sentences and other contrastive sentences will be further examined in the analysis section.

The following examples are illustrations of the above classifications.

(3-13)　我的老师是张先生。
　　　　Wǒ de lǎoshī shì Zhāng xiānshēng.

1SG GEN teacher SHI$_{cop}$ PN honorific.

My teacher is Mr. Zhang.

(3-14) 马是一种动物。

Mǎ shì yī zhǒng dòngwù.

Horse SHI$_{cop}$ one CL animal.

A horse is a type of animal.

Both examples (3-13) and (3-14) fall under the category of equational sentences. However, a key distinction lies in their respective semantic functions. Sentence (3-13) serves to identify a specific sentence constituent (e.g., the subject), allowing for the interchangeability of the two constituents flanking the copula "shi" without altering the meaning or causing syntactic deformation. In contrast, sentence (3-14) functions to denote classification or attribution of a particular constituent. Consequently, in this case, swapping the positions of the two constituents is not permissible.

Considering the word classes of "shi" proposed by different scholars, the following Table 3-1 lists the representative treatments.

Table 3-1 The syntactic classes and semantic interpretations of "shi" proposed by scholars

Scholars	Syntactic classes	Semantic interpretations
Lü (1980), Zhu (1978), Huang (1982)	Main verb	To provide confirmative and linking function between the subject and the post-shi NP/ VP/ADVP/PP/Clause
Shi (2005)	Judgemental verb	To provide judgment (subjective or objective) and evaluation about someone or something
Zhang and Fang (1996)	Verb/Adverb	To provide judgment (subjective or objective) or emphasis towards someone or something

Different from the function of "shi" in copula sentences, the function of "shi" in cleft sentences is to focus the constituent directly following the focus marker "shi". Besides the nature of "shi", crucial differences exist between Chinese copula sentences and cleft sentences, and the differences are unfolded in the following sections.

Chapter 5 will refine the classification of "shi ... de" constructions by distinguishing Chinese cleft sentences from superficially similar structures that differ significantly in function.

3.3 Semantic and Functional Properties of Chinese Cleft Sentences

In the linguistic literature, cleft sentences are associated with at least three different components of meaning: an existential meaning; a specifying (or identifying) meaning; and exhaustiveness (see Percus, 1997; Büring and Križ, 2013; De Veaugh-Geiss et al., 2018). This section introduces and examines the above three components of Chinese cleft sentences.

3.3.1 Exhaustivity

3.3.1.1 Characteristics of exhaustivity

Cleft sentences can be considered exhaustive because they provide a complete and specific focus on a particular element of the sentence. The emphasized element is isolated and highlighted, drawing attention to it and making it the focal point of the sentence. This inherent property of exhaustivity enhances the effectiveness of cleft sentences in conveying precise meaning and reinforcing emphasis on a specific aspect of discourse.

It has long been discussed in the literature that it-clefts give rise to both an existence as well as an exhaustivity inference (see Horn, 1981; Delin, 1992; Abrusán, 2016; Halvorsen, 1977; Percus, 1997; Atlas and Levinson, 1981; Kiss, 1998; Velleman et al., 2012; Büring and Križ, 2013, among others).

Kiss (1998) defined the characteristics of "exhaustivity" in clefts as follows.

(i) The existence of a contextually determined set of alternatives, each of which is a potential candidate for satisfying the predicate of the cleft clause.

(ii) The identification of a single alternative from this set as the exclusive element that fulfills the predicate within the given context.

(iii) The exclusion of all remaining alternatives within the contextually established set, achieved through the negation of each proposition that would result from applying the predicate to any of the other potential alternatives.

Liu and Li (2019) compared the English it-clefts and Chinese focus-making " shi" sentences from two semantic notions — exhaustivity and contrastivity. They concluded that exhaustivity should not be viewed as a separate meaning component encoded in the semantics interpretation of "shi" sentences but is a kind of epiphenomenon derived from contrastivity.

3.3.1.2　The test of exhaustivity

The precondition of making exhaustivity an inevitable criterion of cleft sentences is knowing the way to test it and ensuring every cleft sentence in an actual communication scenario expresses exhaustivity within its context. The following methods are often used to test the exhaust interpretation of sentences.

I. Szabolcsi's (1981) test

The assertion that a non-cleft constituent marked by prominent prosody does not inherently convey exhaustive identification in English is not solely grounded in intuition. Rather, this claim is empirically supported by tests for exhaustive identification developed by Szabolcsi (1981). Szabolcsi's test involves a pair of sentences in which the first sentence contains a focus consisting of two coordinate NPs, and the second sentence differs from the first one only in that one of the coordinate NPs has been dropped. If the first sentence does not entail the second one, in other words, if the second sentence is not among the logical consequence of the first one, the focus of the second sentence expresses exhaustive identification. This method is also called as "failing entailment" test. For example:

(3-15) 是小强和小明要求的。
Shì Xiǎoqiáng hé Xiǎomíng yāoqiú de.
SHI$_{aux}$ Xiaoqiang CONJ Xiaoming require DE$_{ptcl}$.
It was requested by Xiaoqiang and Xiaoming.

(3-16) 是小明要求的。
Shì Xiǎomíng yāoqiú de.
SHI$_{aux}$ Xiaoming requires DE$_{ptcl}$.
It is Xiaoming who required that.

(3-17) 老李是老板以及项目负责人。
Lǎo Lǐ shì lǎobǎn yǐjí xiàngmù fùzérén.
Laoli SHI$_{cop}$ boss CONJ project manager.
Laoli is the boss and the project manager.

(3-18) 老李是老板。
Lǎo Lǐ shì lǎobǎn.
Laoli SHI$_{cop}$ boss.
Laoli is the boss.

By the test, sentence (3-16) is not entailed by (3-15), meaning sentence (3-16) is a sentence with an exhaustive focus. Nevertheless, sentence (3-18) can be logically entailed from sentence (3-17), which means sentence (3-18) is not a sentence with exhaustive focus. Sentences (3-15) and (3-16) are Chinese cleft sentences in the form of "shi...de"; while sentences (3-17) and (3-18) are copula sentences in the form of "bare shi".

II. Paul and Whitman's test (2008)

Paul and Whitman's 2008 test is more convenient and practical, as it allows checking the exhaustivity of focus by simply adding one clause to the original sentence, conveying a similar gist to Szabolcsi 1981. The fundamental idea of the test is that under the condition of exhaustivity, asserting that the property denoted by the presupposition also holds of an entity distinct from the focus of the cleft leads to a contradiction. To quote from his study:

(3-19) It is **Mary** that I gave the book to.

(3-20) ?It is Mary that I gave the book to, and it is also John that I gave the book to.

The same situation is for Chinese cleft sentences.

(3-21) 是小明打破窗户的。

Shì Xiǎomíng dǎpò chuānghu de.

SHIaux Xiaoming break window DEptcl.

It is **Xiaoming** who broke the window.

(3-22) ?[1] 是小明打破窗户的，也是小华打破的。

? shì Xiǎomíng dǎpò chuānghu de, yě shì Xiǎohuá dǎpò de.

? SHI$_{aux}$ Xiaoming break window DE$_{ptcl}$, also SHIaux PN broke DE$_{ptcl}$.

? It is **Xiaoming** who broke the window, it is also **Xiaohua** who did that.

The infelicity of (3-20) and (3-22) provides evidence for the exhaustivity implicated in (3-18) and (3-20).

Ⅲ. Hartmann and Zimmermann's (2007) test

The mechanism of this test is that if a focus-sensitive particle cannot occur in mention-some focus environments, then that particle has (strong) exhaustivity.

This test includes two speakers, one is a teacher, and the other is a student A. According to the reply and context, the test aims to judge whether the student passes the exam.

To put the example in Chinese.

(3-23) Student A:

我通过考试了吗？

---

[1] Symbol "?" before a sentence indicates the example is pragmatically anomalous.

Did I pass the exam?

(a) Teacher's answer:

我不能告诉你,但是小王没通过。

I cannot tell you, but Xiaowang didn't pass.

(b) Teacher's answer:

? 我不能告诉你,但是是小王没通过。

?I cannot tell you, but it is Xiaowang who didn't pass.

Teacher's answer (3-23)(b) fails in mention-some contexts because it presents the focused entity as an exhaustive subset of the situationally relevant set. In other words, the hearer could deduce on the basis of the teacher's answer (3-23) (b) that he had passed the exam by the entailed meaning — there is only one student who did not passed the exam, and that student is Xiaowang. This deduction is originated from the exhaustivity generated by the bare "shi" cleft sentence in answer (3-23)(b). By contrast, the hearer cannot deduce his result of the exam by the canonical declarative sentence expressed in answer (3-23)(a).

3.3.1.3 Pragmatic interpretation of exhaustivity of cleft sentence from Conversational Implicature to Conventional Implicature

As mentioned in Chapter 2, regarding the originality of exhaustivity, the main controversies are centered around its pragmatic and semantic nature. Among others, the pragmatic nature of exhaustivity is supported and discussed in the present study.

Horn (1981) proposed a pragmatic analysis of exhaustive interpretation in it-cleft sentences, suggesting that exhaustiveness arises from the criterion of quantity and is a type of conversational implicature. In simple terms, assuming that speakers provide sufficient information, if a speaker only says, "It's Zhangsan who broke the window," it implies a more informative answer, such as "Zhansan and Lisi broke the window" is a false proposition.

Liu and Li (2019) proposed that using conversational implicature to explain the exhaustive interpretation of cleft sentences in English also faces some problems, such as the difficulty of cancelling exhaustiveness. According to Grice (1975), cancellability is a defining characteristic of conversational implicature. That suggests that conversational implicature may also have difficulty explaining the exhaustive interpretation of cleft sentences.

However, scholars, including Horn himself, proposed a solution for this cancelability issue. For Collins (1991a), exhaustivity is viewed as conventional implicature; or in De Cesare and Garassino's (2015) study, they treat exhaustivity as a *conventionalized conversational implicature*. This categorization displays the originality of exhaustivity and explains its cancellability.

(3-24)　?是小明打破窗户的, 也是小李。
　　　　?It is Xiaoming who broke the window, and it is also Xiaoli.
(3-25)　?我是昨天到北京的, 也是前天。
　　　　?I arrived in Beijing yesterday, and also the day before yesterday.

The oddity of the above two examples indicate the noncancellability.

The gap between the pragmatic and semantic interpretations of exhaustivity can be bridged by the assumption that conversational implicature can become conventionalized (Horn and Bayer, 1984; Levinson, 2000; Morgan, 1978; Searle, 1975). This study applies the pragmatic approach to analyze any relevant topic about the exhaustive interpretation of Chinese cleft sentences. In the latter sections, pragmatic approaches are applied to further analyze the exhaustive inference of the cleft focus.

3.3.1.4　Exhaustivity and alternative set

De Veaugh-Geiss et al. (2018) provided a pragmatic interpretation of exhaustivity in cleft sentences, where the implicature arises from a focus-triggered scalar implicature. They suggested that clefts are a structural mechanism for explicitly marking focus, resulting in more pronounced exhaustivity effects than their regular counterparts.

Regardless of the different approaches by which exhaustivity is achieved, all pragmatic explanations yield similar predictions. Firstly, exhaustivity in clefts can be cancelled, and the speaker can reassert the inference without seeming redundant. Additionally, because the generating mechanism of exhaustive inference is universal, we expect minimal variation across languages. In other words, speakers of all languages should exhibit similar inferential behaviour and derive exhaustivity in clefts.

Disregarding the degree of exhaustivity, the exhaustive interpretation of cleft sentences is encoded similarly to the particle "only". Let us quote some examples of "only" sentences:

(3-26)　John only got his degree from **Cal State** (X)

　　　　The alternative set for X could be {Standford, USC, UCLA, Cal State}

In this case, not all alternatives are excluded; instead, only the "stronger" ones in some non-logical/pragmatic sense. Exclusion upward along a scale reflects some (non-logical) ordering relation. The scalar presupposition encodes a qualitative judgment: there are (sufficiently) many better alternatives.

(3-27)　老师：谁叫你来的？

　　　　Teacher: Who asked you to come?

　　　　(a) 学生：是**班长**（X）叫我来的。

　　　　Student: It is the **class representative** who asked me to come.

　　　　(b) ? 学生：是**您妈妈**叫我来的。

　　　　?Student: It is **your mom** who asked me to come.

　　　　(c) ? 学生：是**女同学**叫我来的。

　　　　?Student: It is **a female classmate** who asked me to come.

The alternative set for X could be {your mom, a female classmate, the class representative}. Disregarding the definiteness of the noun phrases falling within the domain of focus, we conclude the acceptability of answers (a) to (c) relays on the non-logical/ pragmatic sense of the question under its certain communication context.

3.3.1.5 Exhaustivity and scalar implicature

Grice (1975) proved the presence of a scalar implicature by stating examples like the following.

(3-28) Susan had sushi or noodles for supper.
(3-29) Susan didn't have sushi and noodles for supper.
(3-30) Susan had some of the cookies for supper.
(3-31) Susan didn't have all of the cookies for supper.

Sentences (3-28) and (3-30) are infelicitous assertions unless their implicatures (3-29) and (3-31) are satisfied. Horn (1972) further identified additional tests to detect scalar implicatures, one of which involves the use of "suspender clauses", as shown in (3-32).

(3-32) Susan had sushi or noodles, and possibly Susan even had sushi and noodles.

According to Horn (1972), the acceptability of continuations of a sentence Φ with phrases like "and possibly…even ψ" is contingent upon the negation of ψ being a scalar implicature of Φ. The acceptability of (3-34) thus confirms the presence of the exhaustive implicature in (3-28), which is characterized by the "not-and" relationship.

Gazdar (1979) proposed a precise mechanism for computing scalar implicatures, building on the notion of a quantitative scale introduced by Horn (1972). This mechanism applies specifically to sentences Φ where an expression from a quantitative scale α appears outside the scope of any logical operator, as described by Gazdar (1979), Atlas and Levinson (1981), and Levinson (2000). Let's formulate the exhaustive interpretation here:

$$\text{Sentence: } \Phi = f(\alpha)$$

Gazdar's mechanism explains the decoding of an implicature for sentence Φ suppose that α is not the maximal item on its quantitative scale set Q.

Based on the given information, replace a word α with the word that follows it (denoted as α' who possesses stronger semantic features) in a given context Φ, to form a new expression:

$$\psi = f(\alpha')$$

This new expression ψ is then used to generate scalar implicatures of Φ using the epistemic certainty operator K, which expresses the speaker's certainty about the argument of K.

The scalar implicatures of Φ are expressed as "$K\neg\psi$" for any ψ that can be derived using the aforementioned mechanism. This can be paraphrased as "The speaker is certain that ψ is false", where the speaker expresses certainty about the negation of ψ.

To put this test into the exhaustive interpretation of Chinese cleft sentences.

(3-33)　是小明要求的。

　　　　Shì Xiǎomíng yāoqiú de.

　　　　SHI$_{aux}$ Xiaoming request DE$_{ptcl}$.

　　　　It is Xiaoming who required that.

(3-34)　? 是小强和小明要求。

　　　　? Shì Xiǎoqiáng hé Xiǎomíng yāoqiú.

　　　　? It is Xiaoqiang CONJ Xiaoming required.

　　　　? It is Xiaoqiang and Xiaoming who required that.

The infelicity is elicited by the exhaustivity of Chinese cleft sentences. In the following sections, the exhaustivity of cleft sentences is explained by Grice's Cooperative Principles and Gazdar's scalar implicature.

Grice's maxims, also known as Gricean maxims, are a set of four principles proposed by philosopher H.P. The essence of the Cooperative Principle is to make your conversational contribution such as is required, at the stage at which it occurs, by the accepted purpose or direction of the talk exchange in which you are engaged. By this principle, Grice described how people communicate effectively in conversation.

For Quantity maxim, Grice proposed two sub-maxims.

(i) Make your contribution as informative as is required (for the current purpose of the exchange).

(ii) Do not make your contribution more informative than is required.

The quantity maxim suggests speakers make their contribution as informative as is required. This principle suggests that speakers should provide enough information in their contributions to be informative but not overly verbose or excessively detailed. It means providing the right amount of information needed to convey the intended meaning without leaving out crucial details or providing unnecessary information that may lead to confusion.

Let us go back to example (3-33) by stating the fact as: "It is Xiaoming who required", from both speaker's and the hearer's point of view, the speaker obeys the quantity maxim by choosing the exact amount of information needed by the listener's encoding procedure regarding the current utterance. The hearer also assumes that what the speaker provides is the right amount of information he can provide at the current stage. Under the guidance of the quantity maxim, the speaker cannot imply the interpretation of (3-34) from sentence (3-33); this explanation also elicits the exhaustive interpretation of the Chinese cleft sentence.

Let us check the suitability of Gazdar's Scalar Implicature to the exhaustive reading of the cleft sentence by (3-33) and (3-34) again.

The formulation of the sentence (3-34) is "$\Phi = f(\alpha)$", with "α" representing the semantically weaker item on the quantitative scale set Q. Sentence (3-33) is formulated as $\psi = f(\alpha')$, with α' representing the semantically strong item of the set. So, the alternative set could be {Xiaoqiang and Xiaoming, Xiaoming}. Sentence (3-33) cannot imply (3-34); in other words, the implicature generated from (3-33) is:

$$\Phi = f(\alpha) +> \text{``}K \neg \psi = \neg f(\alpha')\text{''}$$

Hearers are not sure about the certainty of the sentence (3-34).

It is tested that both from the perspectives of quantity maxim or scalar implicature, exhaustivity of Chinese cleft sentences can be explained from the pragmatic perspective, and its interpretations are in line with Szabolcsi's (1981) test.

3.3.2 Specificational meaning

Specificational and predicational sentences deliver different semantic functions of sentences. Declerck (1988) claimed that a specificational sentence is one whose semantic function is to specify a value for a variable, while a predicational sentence predicates a property of the subject NP.

It is generally assumed that English cleft sentences are specificational constructions (Akmajian, 1970; Halvorsen, 1977; Heggie, 1988); however, few researchers suggested that certain clefts are predicational structures (Ball, 1977, 1978; Declerck,1988). For example, Ball (1977, 1978) proposed that an English cleft can be interpreted as a predicational construction when the clefted constituent (i.e., focus) is "an indefinite NP of the form DET ADJ N", as in the following example.

(3-35)　It was **a simple and uneventful life** that Schubert lived. [NY Times 2/19/78]

A structurally similar Chinese example is shown here:

(3-36)　我是在一个风很安静的夜晚离开的。(from the movie *A Chinese Odyssey*.

Wǒ shì zài yí gè fēng hěn ānjìng de yèwǎn líkāi de.
1SG SHI$_{aux}$ PREP one-CL wind very quiet DE$_{modi}$ night leave PRT.

In **a night with a gentle breeze**, I left.

The focus of the sentence is " a night with a gentle breeze" in the form of "DET ADJ N" . However, this sentence is a cleft sentence and specificational in nature with the referent of the focus constituent showing specificity. To explain the specificational nature of this sentence.

Firstly, the above sentence is reversible, treating "shi" as the pivot, although the original and the reversed sentences have different foci and functions. The reversed sentence of (3-35) is:

(3-37)　在一个风很安静的夜晚离开的是我。
　　　　Zài yí gè fēng hěn ānjìng de yèwǎn líkāi de shì wǒ.
　　　　PREP one-CL wind very quiet DE$_{modi}$ night leave DE$_{nomi}$ SHI$_{cop}$ 1SG.
　　　　It is **me** who left in a night with a gentle breeze.

It is noteworthy that the grammatical categories of "shi" and "de" differ between examples (3-36) and (3-37). Sentence (3-37) is changed from a cleft sentence to a pseudo-cleft[①] sentence, switching the focus from adjunct " a night with a gentle breeze" to the argument of the sentence "me". This reversibility of sentence (3-36) suggests that it is a specificational sentence, for the reversibility of the predicational sentence is not felicitous (Niimura, 2007).

Secondly, and most importantly, the information structure of the sentence determines whether it is a cleft sentence. The relationship between the subject and predicate is mainly known as "topic-comment" for predicational sentences. However, for clefts, there is an (event-)existential presupposition "I left at (some moment)", please see the existential presupposition through the following Russellian analysis.

$\exists x$ [Time (x)] and $\forall y$[Time(y)$\rightarrow$ y = x] and I left at (x)]

The existential reading of the above formula is: There is one moment and not any other moment at which I left.

The focus is an exhaustive element (x) that can be inserted into the presupposition and, thus, makes a final assertion presented by the whole

---

① The structure "...de shi..." (in which "de" represents a nominal clause with the element before "de" usually taking the form of a verb phrase) is widely considered as the form of Chinese pseudocleft sentences by Chinese scholars (cf. Fang 1995; Huang and Fawcett, 1996).

sentence (3-36).

Thirdly, according to Hedberg (1990), if a sentence is a predicational cleft sentence, then its paraphrase can be shown by a simple predicational copula sentence. To cite one example from Hedberg's study, sentence (3-38) is paraphrased into (3-39) without any grammatical error or semantic infelicity.

(3-38)　It was **an odd televised ceremony** that I watched from my living room and a touching one, marking the difficult transition the Carrs had made couple to family, formally introducing a child into the world. (Goodman, 1985, *Keeping in touch*, p.194)

(3-39)　The televised ceremony that I watched from my living room was an odd one and a touching one.

To conduct the test on the Chinese counterpart by paraphrasing example (3-36):

(3-40)　？我离开的是在一个风很安静的夜晚。
　　　　Wǒ líkāi de shì zài yí gè fēng hěn ānjìng de yèwǎn.
　　　　1SG leave DE$_{ptcl}$ SHI$_{aux}$ PREP one-CL wind very quiet DE$_{modi}$ night.

Sentence (3-40) is another type of Chinese " … de shi … " pseudo-cleft sentence, but different from (3-37), (3-40) is not grammatically correct. The reason is that, different from Chinese cleft sentences, Chinese pseudo-cleft sentences do not accept adjunct constituents as the sentence's focus.

Based on the above observation, Chinese cleft sentences, even the one with "an indefinite NP of the form DET ADJ N" as its focus (i.e., that of example (3-36), are considered specificational constructions.

The crucial characteristic for specificational meaning is that some copula sentences and cleft sentences project a universally quantified restricted or existentially presupposed set, which is inherent in the semantics of a definite/

identifiable noun phrase and a referential member that specifies the set. In contrast, a predicational sentence is "about" something and usually explains or describes the subject's nature, attribution, or characteristics. The subject of the predicational sentence refers to some individual, and the predicate states that individual's property and attribute. In specificational sentences, the referent of the post-*shi* noun phrase is the entity that meets a condition denoted by the pre-*shi* noun phrase. Higgins (1979) suggested that specificational sentences involve a "value-variable" relation — "the heading of a list provides a 'variable', thereby delimiting a certain domain, to which the items on the list conform as 'values' of that variable." He argued that specificational sentences do not hold a predication relationship since "The whole notion of being 'about' something is alien to a list" (Higgins, 1979, p. 155).

3.3.3 Existential meaning — the existential presupposition

The cleft clause, the second part of the cleft sentence, not only carries an exhaustiveness condition for the clefted constituent but also expresses an existential presupposition. This can be observed from the fact that the proposition with existentially quantified meaning in the cleft clause remains unchanged even when subjected to negation, questioning, or used as an antecedent in a conditional statement, as demonstrated in Chierchia and McConnell-Ginet (1990).

The existential presupposition is a term used in linguistics and philosophy to refer to a type of presupposition, which is an assumption or belief that a speaker assumes to be true or takes for granted when making a statement. Existential presupposition specifically deals with the implicit assumption or presupposition that something exists or is real. Cleft sentences convey information that is commonly understood by presuppositions. This presupposition, triggered at the sentence level rather than the NP/DP level, is associated with the proposition that someone has the property of some action expressed by the cleft clause rather than the existence of the cleft constituent. The presupposition can be described as an open proposition, as in the following example.

(3-41) Susan is the one who stole the cookies.
Presupposition: There is someone (x) who stole the cookies.

Kripke (2009) asserted that many elements of presupposition are linked to prior discourse or contextual elements, in contrast to the traditional approach of assigning presuppositions to each clause independently.

Treating presupposition as anaphora is helpful in constructing representations of presupposition, especially in the framework of *Discourse Representation Theory* (Kamp, 1981), empirical evidence for the anaphoricity of cleft presupposition of English cleft sentences is proposed by Delin (1992, p. 289).

(i) Elements that are ambiguous between an anaphoric and an emphatic use take on their anaphoric reading when placed within an it-cleft presupposition.

(ii) It-cleft presuppositions enable the anaphoric relation upon which contrast depends to be established in contexts where information that is simply given does not have the same effect.

(iii) Information placed within an it-cleft presupposition appears to remind rather than inform, regardless of its objective status in the discourse.

Based on contemporary theories of presupposition, beginning with Van der Sandt's 1989 work, it is now widely recognized that presupposition functions as a type of propositional anaphora. This means that the presupposed proposition relies on a previous proposition in the discourse context, similar to how definite descriptions or pronouns function as anaphors. In some cases, an antecedent may not be available at the time of utterance, and one may need to be constructed or accommodated in the context before the presupposing sentence can be adequately understood.

To indicate the existential nature of the presupposition of Chinese cleft sentences, here cite several examples.

(3-42) 是小明打破窗户的。
Shì Xiǎomíng dǎpò chuānghu de.
SHI$_{aux}$ Xiaoming break window DE$_{ptcl}$.
It is **Xiaoming** who broke the window.
Presupposition: (There is) Someone (x) broke the window.

The existential nature of the presupposition of cleft sentences is widely accepted by scholars, and the existential presupposition is an open proposition. Cleft sentences provide a value (i.e., focus) for the variable (x) of the open proposition (i.e., presupposition). For example, in (3-42), the possible set of variables (x) could be {Xiaoming, Zhangsan, Wangwu, Lisi}, and "Xiaoming" is the right value under the context and background knowledge of both the hearer and speaker when the sentence is uttered, so it is assigned to the presupposition making an assertion.

There are cases in Chinese cleft data focusing on the adjunct of the verbs. For this type, the nature of presupposition is still existential, but different from argument-focus cleft sentences, the presuppositions of adjunct cleft sentences are "event-existential presupposition" with the name "event-existential" borrowed from Huang (1987). "Event" is considered a second-order entity by Lyon (1977, 442-445) — "the second-order entities are events, processes/activities, and states". The argument-focus clefts show existential presupposition by automatically supplementing the "missing" argument with a "有 (have)" from the listener, while the event-existential presupposition shows the existence of action through a proposition in which the focus constituent is replaced by its hypernym defining the semantic set presupposed by the sentence. The following is one example of the adjunct focus cleft sentence.

(3-43) 我是昨天到北京的。
Wǒ shì zuótiān dào Běijīng de.

1SG SHI$_{aux}$ yesterday arrive Beijing DE$_{ptcl}$.
It was **yesterday** when I arrived in Beijing.
Presupposition: I arrived in Beijing (when X).
Focus: yesterday
Focus domain: NP

To compare the cleft sentences with sentence-focus emphatic sentences (or named "propositional assertion" by Paul and Whitman, 2008), the distribution of assertion and presupposition is different.

(3-44) 他是一定会对你好一辈子的。(Liu and Li, 2019)
Tā shì yídìng huì duì nǐ hǎo yíbèizi de.
He SHI$_{aux}$ definitely will treat you well his whole life DE$_{ptcl}$.
He will definitely treat you well for his whole life.
Presupposition: null
Focus: He will definitely treat you well for his whole life.

The presupposition in the above emphatic " shi … de" sentence is a null proposition, and the focus falls on the whole sentence. Same as the emphatic "shi … de" sentences, "shi … de" copula sentences demonstrate different types of presuppositions as Chinese cleft sentences. This feature can be used as the criterion to distinguish Chinese cleft sentences from other non-cleft "shi … de" sentences. The detailed distinguishing process is displayed in chapter 5.

3.4 The Syntactic and Functional Role of "shi" in Cleft Sentences

Linguists hold varying perspectives regarding the syntactic status and functions of "shi". These perspectives can be classified into the following categories.

3.4.1 "Shi" as a main verb/ copula of the sentence

This category claims that "shi" is the main verb in the cleft sentence. Scholars who hold this view are Hashimoto (1969), Li and Thompson (1981), Ross (1983), Tang (1983), and Zhu (1978).

Hashimoto (1969) suggested that "shi" should be treated as a verb based on its unique distribution. She said that "shi" can be negated like any other verb. In Chinese, only verbs can be negated; hence she did not exclude "shi" from the verb category. She treated "shi" as the main verb and clefts/pseudo-clefts as the copulative sentence.

Ross (1983) treated "shi" as a main verb and believed that the cleft sentence is a special case of the equational sentence because "shi" denotes an indirect equational relation. To some extent, the clause after "shi" determines the elements before it.

The problems of this approach lie in the following aspects.

(i) Scholars holding this approach prefer to treat cleft sentences as equational or copula sentences whose function is different from that of cleft sentences.

(ii) If "shi" is indeed a verb, as this approach claims, then why can't it appear before the object? This approach cannot solve these problems.

3.4.2 "Shi" as a focus marker

The second solution treats "shi" as a focus marker functionally in the cleft sentence (Shi, 2005; Teng, 1979; Zhang and Fang, 1996). "Shi" has no substantial meaning, and the cleft sentence is a simple sentence. The scholars thought that "shi" was free to be placed before any constituent before the predicate and did not affect the structure of the original proposition. Hence, the cleft sentence remained a simple sentence.

However, there are four subcategories of the word category of "shi".

The first one displays that "shi" is an independent focus marker in the cleft sentence; the other three consider "shi" as a focus marker belonging to different syntactic categories.

(i) "Shi" as a specialized focus marker. Fang (1995) proposed that "shi" is originally a surplus element in the spoken language, but it has a significant effect in the written language. "Shi" is not an essential element in the sequential syntactic structure of a sentence having some substantial meaning, so it can be left out. Teng (1979) held the view that "shi" in the cleft sentence is a marker specialized for indicating the focus. By inserting "shi" before the focus of a sentence, the original sentence becomes a cleft sentence.

(ii) "Shi" as a focus marker having the status of an adverb on a par with negation and modals. This view is proposed by Huang (1982), he claimed that "'shi' is a focus operator which has the attribute of an adverb on a par with negation and modals" (p. 213). Its status as an adverb explains why it cannot directly focalize the element behind a verb (e.g., in example 3-50), but at the same time, it can be inserted before any constituent in front of the predicate and then focalize it without any other sentence-order alteration. For example:

(3-45) Basic sentence: 他打我。
Tā dǎ wǒ.
3SG hit 1SG.
He **hit me**.

(3-46) cleft sentence: 他是打我。
Tā shì dǎ wǒ.
3SG SHI$_{aux}$ hit 1SG.
(i) It is **me** who was hit by him.
(ii) He **hit** me.

(3-47) cleft sentence: 是他打我。
Shì tā dǎ wǒ.
SHI$_{aux}$ 3SG hit 1SG.

It is **he** who hit me.

(3-48)   * 他打是我。

   *Tā dǎ shì wǒ.

   3SG hit SHI$_{cop/aux}$ 1SG.

(iii) "Shi" as a focus marker having the status of a verb. Xu and Li (1993) assumed that "shi" is a verb with the function of a focus marker. In other words, the function of "shi" is to denote the focus. At the same time, since "shi" is a verb, it must obey the rule of being a verb.

(iv) "Shi" as a focus marker and a raising auxiliary. Huang has written two papers about the status of "shi" (Huang, 1982, 1988). Differing from his earlier statement, Huang (1988) considered "shi" in the cleft sentence to be a subject raising auxiliary like "可能 (may)," "应该 (should or ought to)", "会 (may)" in Chinese, or as "seem" in English.

"Shi" in the clefts is allowed to appear before the subject if the subject is not raised; or between the subject and predicate if the subject is raised. The subject-raising in the clefts, which contain an auxiliary "shi" is not obligatory but optional, whereas "会 (hui; may)" in the sentence "这本书会涨价 (The price of this book is to raise)" has to be raised (Huang, 1988).

Let us make further illustration by the following example.

(3-49)   是我打了他。

   Shì wǒ dǎ le tā.

   SHI$_{aux}$ 1SG hit LE$_{aspc}$ 3SG.

   It is **me** who hit him.

Huang (1988) considered "shi" in cleft sentences as a raising auxiliary that allows the raising of the subject. According to Huang (1988), the deep structure of the sentence (3-49) as Figure 3-2.

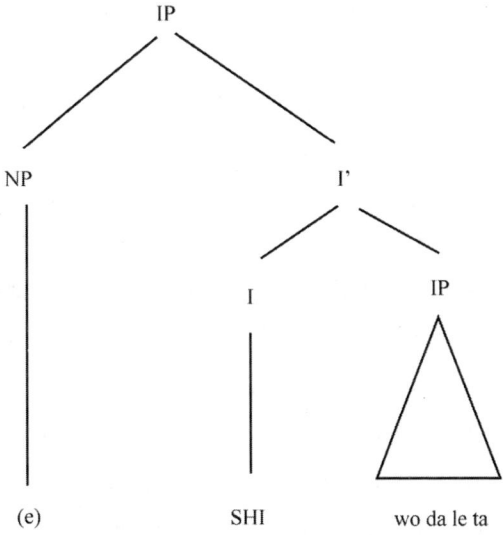

Figure 3-2 Syntactic tree diagram of sentence (3-49)

The subject "我 (wo)" in the clause "我打了他 (wo da le ta)" is raised to the spec of the IP, "shi" here is the auxiliary which allows the movement of the subject, hence it is called the raising auxiliary. The omission of the auxiliary is acceptable in these sentences. But one thing has to be mentioned in particular: although the subject of the clause can be raised before the raising auxiliary, the movement does change the focus of the sentence. Before the movement, the focus of the sentence "是我打了他 (It was me who hit him)" is the subject "我 (wo; me)"; the focus of the moved sentence "我是打了他 (I hit him, indeed)" is the whole clause "我打了他 (I hit him)". In other words, the raising potential of the subject determines the possible location of "shi" both before the subject and after it. In Chinese "shi" sentences, if "shi" is located in the preceding position of the main verb of the sentence, very likely, it is a sentence-emphatic sentence, and the auxiliary "shi" is often stressed prosodically. To summarize, in the sentence "SHI_{aux} wo da LE ta" if the subject of the clause is moved, the sentence is an emphatic one; if not, it is a cleft sentence.

The advantage of treating "shi" as an auxiliary is that the rule for the distribution of "shi" is thereafter restricted. The auxiliary can be positioned before the predicate but not behind the predicate or prepositions. "Shi" is required to obey these restrictions. The preposition-object structure belongs to the predicate; hence, "shi" and other auxiliaries cannot appear behind these preposition-object structures. That "shi" can be put before or behind the words "可能 (keneng; maybe)", and "应该 (yinggai; should)" is because these auxiliaries are similar to the auxiliary "shi", which can be distributed as the head word of the parent clause or the subclause.

The present study analyses "shi" as a focus marker with its syntactic class as a raising auxiliary. It can be put at the initial position of the sentence; and functionally, as with other auxiliaries of Chinese, it acts as a modal verb by, for example, enhancing the confirmative mood of the sentence. This distinguishes clefts from the equational sentences in which "shi" is acting as the copula; and explains the function of the assertive mood of the clefts; thirdly, it explains why "shi" cannot be placed between verb and object to highlight the object of the sentence.

3.5 The Syntactic and Functional Role of "de" in Cleft Sentences

Similar to the research on "shi", the analysis of "de" in "shi ... de" cleft sentences exhibits considerable variation across different scholars. The previous approaches to "de" should be summarized generally into the following criteria.

I. Modification-marker approach

The modifier-marker approach tries to assume "de" in the "shi ... de" sentences as a modification marker. Ross (1983) included possessive "de", adjective "de", relative clause "de", and appositive clause "de" into the same classification of "modification-marker". Simpson and Wu (1999) included "nominalizer" and "determiner" in this approach. In addition, they reanalyze "de" from category D to category T and make it a past tense morpheme base-generated as the head of TP.

II. Structural particle approach

Unlike Simpson and Wu (1999), Chu (1979) did not suggest that "de" can be a past tense marker. He proposed that "de" is a particle that can contain the presupposition. The presupposition of a cleft sentence is defined as the string preceding "de" except the focus. Teng (1979) and Tang (1983) regarded "de" as a particle, and it occurs independently from the subject and the predicate.

Zhu (1980), Yuan (2003), Cao and Bao (2018), and Cao (2019) held the idea that as a structural particle, the primary function of "de" is to transfer the predicate of the sentence into a nominalized constituent. This approach is in line with treating Chinese cleft sentences as copula sentences ignoring the semantic presupposition and the focus type of Chinese clefts.

III. "de" as an aspectual marker

Song (1981), Wang (2003), and other scholars considered "de" as the aspectual marker of the cleft sentence, representing the finished status of the action. However, "de" can also appear in sentences describing unfinished action, such as simple present and present continuous. Another problem with this approach is that it cannot explain the co-occurrence of both "de" and other aspectual markers, such as "le" or "guo".

IV. "de" as a mood particle

Teng (1979), Tang (1983), Chiu (1993), and Chu (1979) treated "de" in Chinese cleft sentences as mood particle. Chu (1979) proposed that "de" is a particle and can contain the presupposition. Teng (1979) and Tang (1983) regarded "de" as a particle, and it occurs independently from the subject and the predicate. Cao and Bao (2018) proposed that the particle nature of "de" is driven by its evidential function: to confirm an action instead of reporting an event.

Furthermore, "de" can also function as an indicator of tense or mood in a sentence, a perspective supported by the research of Liu and Cheng (2021). The analysis of the multifaceted use of "de" aligns with Liu's earlier work in 2018 on the concept of a parasitic category.

However, Liu and Cheng's (2021) study fails to differentiate between emphatic sentences with "shi...de" and cleft sentences with "shi...de". In their investigation, the former is categorized as cleft sentences with a broad focus domain, while the latter pertains to clefts with a narrower focus domain. They indicate that in cleft sentences with a broad focus, "de" serves as a mood particle, intensifying the confirming tone of the sentence. Conversely, in cleft sentences with a narrow focus, "de" functions both as an aspectual marker and a mood particle.

This study shares some common ground with Liu and Cheng's perspective in recognizing "de" as a mood particle aimed at reinforcing confirmation and assertion. However, distinct from emphatic sentences with "shi...de", this study maintains that, in cleft sentences, "de" as a mood particle heightens the evidentiality of the existential presupposition. As a particle, "de" does not contribute any specific content to the presupposition, thus remaining detached from the presupposition of Chinese cleft sentences.

3.6 Summary

Based on the properties of Chinese cleft sentences mentioned in this chapter, basic distinctions are made between Chinese cleft sentences and non-cleft "shi ... de" sentences, which are summarized in the subsequent Table 3-2.

Table 3-2 Distinctions between Chinese "shi...de" sentences

Types		Semantic functions	Presupposition	SHI	DE	Exhaustivity
Copula sentences	Explanatory	Predicational	+	copula	Modifier	−
	Attributive	Predicational	+	copula	Modifier	−
	Classifying	Predicational	+	copula	Modifier/nominalizer	−
	Identifying	Specificational	+	copula	Modifier	−
Emphatic sentences		Predicational	−	auxiliary	Mood Particle	−
Cleft sentences		Specificational	+ (Existentially propositional presupposition)	Raising auxiliary	Particle +tense/aspect marker	+

As an essential means of focus expression, cleft sentences may establish the correlation between information structures and focus and their syntactic representations as well as their identifiability to the speaker. There are some conclusions already made in languages as English, such as the scale of the acceptability of the topic provided by different scholars (e.g., Lambrecht, 1994; Gundel et al., 1993); however, this rule is not testified either as a necessary or universal principle for all languages. This study discusses the identifiability of referents of topic and focus constituents, the definiteness of their grammatical constituents, and the distributive feature of the information structure of Chinese cleft sentences.

Previous studies on the information structure of Chinese cleft sentences have generally examined various mechanisms of focus realization, with cleft constructions in Chinese representing just one such method.

This book aims to take Chinese cleft sentences as the sole starting point and examines the internal distribution and configuration of their information structure from both sentential and discourse perspectives.

Chapter 4

Theoretical Framework

This chapter introduces the essential theories and concepts of the present study. In Section 1, an overview of information structure (including the definitions and basic concepts such as topic and focus, etc.) and the research findings of Chinese information structure are presented. In Section 2, Lambrecht's classification of focus structures is introduced, serving as the theoretical foundation for the present study. The specific configurations of information structure associated with different types constitute essential criteria for identifying cleft sentences. Section 3 illustrates the relationship and differences between definiteness, referentiality, and identifiability. Section 4 provides a clear explanation of the whole mechanism of the model of identifiability proposed by Lambrecht. Modifications of the model are made to adapt to the semantic and discoursal features of Chinese. Section 5 interprets identifiability from a cognitive perspective. This chapter provides new angle to reconsider the differences between Chinese cleft sentences and the other "shi ... de" sentences from the perspective of the information structure.

4.1 Information Structure: An Overview

The information structure of languages refers to how languages convey and organize information within sentences or utterances. It involves how languages express the topic, focus, and background information in communication. Different languages have different ways of structuring and conveying information, and understanding these structures can help in analyzing and interpreting meaning in communication.

Prince (1981) provides the concept of "information packaging" as the following:

"(Information packaging is) the tailoring of an utterance by a sender to meet the particular assumed needs of the intended receiver. That is, information packaging in natural language reflects the sender's hypotheses about the receiver's assumptions and beliefs, and strategies." (p. 224)

Several points may be taken care of in this definition, which together produce the whole process of information delivery.

Firstly, information structure bridges the addresser and the addressee.

Secondly, "hypotheses about the receiver's assumptions" are hypotheses about the states of the mental representations of the referents or concepts of linguistic expressions in the mind of the receiver at the moment of utterance.

Thirdly, there are strategies during the delivery of information. It is crucial to notice here that the study of information structure is not concerned with the lexical and propositional content of the sentence constituent, but with the way such content is transmitted. The psychological and mental thinking between the addresser and addressee is transmitted by particular grammatical strategies.

The studies of information explore the mutual relationship between the interpretation of words or sentences in given conversational contexts and the discourse circumstances under which given pieces of propositional information are expressed.

Lambrecht (1994) proposed the definition of "information structure" in his book:

"That component of sentence grammar in which propositions as conceptual representations of states of affairs are paired with lexicogrammatical structures in accordance with the mental states of interlocutors who use and interpret these structures as units of information in given discourse contexts." (p. 5)

Lambrecht's theories of information structure are applied and discussed through the whole study.

4.1.1 Important concepts of information structure

The key concepts of information structure proposed by Lambrecht (1994) include the following aspects.

(i) Presupposition and assertion, which have to do with the structuring of propositions into portions that a speaker assumes an addressee already knows or does not yet know, respectively.

(ii) Identifiability and activation, which have to do with a speaker's assumptions about the statuses of the mental representations of discourse referents in the addressee's mind at the time of an utterance; although identifiability and activation are independent cognitive categories, identifiability having to do with knowledge while activation has to do with consciousness, the two correlate with each other in certain predictable ways. A referent being activated entails that it is identifiable. The detailed differences and categories of activation are discussed in the following sections.

(iii) Topic and focus, which have to do with a speaker's assessment of the relative predictability vs. unpredictability of the relations between propositions and their elements in given discourse situations. (p. 6)

One important clarification must be made here: the term "presupposition" as used by Lambrecht (1994) is a pragmatic concept and should be distinguished from other types of presupposition.

Semantic presupposition and pragmatic presupposition are two concepts in linguistics and philosophy that refer to different types of implied meanings in language.

Semantic presupposition refers to the implied meaning that is inherently embedded within the proposition itself, independent of the communicative context. In contrast, pragmatic presupposition pertains to the meaning implied by the speaker's intentions and the specific context of communication. A detailed explanation is provided below.

I. Semantic presupposition

In Huang's (2012) "The Oxford Dictionary of Pragmatics", the semantic presupposition is much like an entailment.①

The semantic presupposition is dependent on the structure of an utterance. The truth value of the semantic presupposition is not influenced by the negation of the sentence or utterance. For example, A and B are discussing their mutual friend C.

(4-1)　A: He knows that the capital of New Zealand is Auckland.

A's presupposition "the capital of New Zealand is Auckland" is a presupposition failure for it is false. This negation of the sentence "He doesn't know that the capital of New Zealand is Auckland" does not make A's presupposition a different one. The presupposition is a semantic one here.

II. Pragmatic presupposition

Jackendoff (1972, p. 230) considered the pragmatic presupposition to be the information of one sentence that is assumed by the speaker to be shared by him/her and the hearer. Karttunen (1973) defined the pragmatic presupposition as follows: "To presuppose a sentence in the pragmatic sense is to take its truth for granted and to assume that the audience does the same".

Huang (2014) distinguished the two types of presupposition in his book. According to him, the pragmatic presupposition refers to the given information which is "(the) part of the (relevant) context (or common ground), and in particular, the speaker's commitment slate in which the sentence is uttered" (p. 85).

In his study, he called the cleft sentence one of the presupposition

---

　　① Lyons (1977, p. 85) pointed out that entailment is "a relation that holds between P and Q where P and Q are variables standing for propositions such that if the truth of Q necessarily follows from the truth of P (and the falsity of Q necessarily follows from the falsity of P), then P entails Q."

triggers that engender presuppositions by their structural forms. To quote one example from Huang (2014).

(4-2) It was Baird who invented television.
>>[1] Someone invented television.

The distinct configurations of information structure corresponding to various types serve as crucial criteria for the identification of cleft constructions. The detailed discussion will be unfolded in Chapter 5.

Keenan (1972) provided a series of examples to demonstrate that natural language indeed contains two types of presuppositions: semantic presupposition and pragmatic presupposition. His examples for each type differ significantly. All examples illustrating logical/semantic presuppositions are drawn from English, whereas all examples of pragmatic presuppositions come from exotic languages. This distinction leads to the conclusion that pragmatic presuppositions depend on "certain culturally defined conditions" (Keenan, 1972, p. 46) and are context-driven.

Stalnaker (1973) distinguished between two ways of treating presuppositions. From a semantic point of view being a presupposition is a relation between a sentence and a proposition; whereas from a pragmatic point of view being a presupposition is a relation between the speaker and a proposition. Stalnaker argued in favour of the second analysis, which he found more general and intuitive than the first. More specifically, he claimed that "a proposition presupposed by a sentence in a technical semantic sense provides a reason for requiring it be presupposed in the pragmatic sense whenever the sentence is used" (p. 452). The reason why he took pragmatic presupposition as the more intuitive form is that pragmatic presupposition explains the presupposition failure caused by semantic presupposition. Presupposition failure occurs when the proposition assumed to be true is in fact false. In Stalnaker's pragmatic account of presupposition, the example (4-1) is not problematic. He treated the presupposition failure as a non-

---

[1] This symbol means a proposition "presupposes" the other proposition.

catastrophic one.[①] There is a close relationship between semantic and pragmatic presuppositions. An utterance of a sentence that has a semantic presupposition is associated with a pragmatic presupposition (Sudo, 2014).

Let us return to the important concepts of information structure. As mentioned at the beginning of this section, the important concepts of information structure proposed by Lambrecht (1994) are applied in this study. In the previous literature, various terms are given to these concepts by different schools. The terminology for information dichotomy includes:

(i) theme-rheme (Ammann, 1925; Halliday, 1967; Mathesius, 1929);

(ii) topic-comment (Reinhart, 1981);

(iii) topic-focus (Sgall et.al, 1973);

(iv) presupposition-focus (Lambrecht, 1994; Jackendoff, 1972);

(v) background-focus (Chafe, 1976; Jacobs, 1982);

(vi) old/ given-new information (Chafe, 1976; Halliday, 1967);

(vii) open proposition-focus (Prince, 1981);

(viii) notional subject-notional predicate (Kiss, 1995).

Regardless of the various terminologies, most of the researchers agreed that the defining criteria of the partition are contrastivity/contrastiveness and informativeness, and the terminologies depart from different perspectives.

For example, Chafe (1976) paid attention to the givenness of constituents of a sentence. As a type of activation in the consciousness of the speaker and hearer, givenness initiates the discussion of a scale of givenness. Several givenness and activation hierarchies are proposed by scholars, such as the *Scale of Assumed Familiarity* (Prince, 1981), the *Givenness Hierarchy* (Gundel et al, 1993), and Lambrecht's (1994) system of identifiability and activation. Lambrecht's system of identifiability and activation is based on Prince's scale. They categorized the familiarity (in Prince, 1981) and unidentifiability (in Lambrecht, 1994) of the referents in the sentence

---

① Failure is catastrophic if it prevents a thing from performing its primary task—in the semantic case making an evaluable claim. Non-catastrophic presupposition failure then becomes the phenomenon of a sentence still making an evaluable claim despite presupposing a falsehood.

according to their givenness or newness to both the communicators and the discourse. For example, the referent known by the speaker but not by the hearer is a brand-new one (in Prince, 1981) and inactive (in Lambrecht, 1994). The analytical framework adopted in the present study is grounded in Lambrecht's (1994) model, which will be elaborated upon in subsequent sections.

Gundel et al. (1993) proposed six cognitive statuses of referents that were evoked by relevant determiners and pronouns. This scale relates the givenness and the grammatical constituent (i.e., demonstratives, pronouns, etc.) together directly. One of the tasks of the present study is to check the identifiability and definiteness (i.e., "familiarity" in Prince, 1981) of focus and topic constituents of Chinese cleft sentences. The identifiability model of the present study is mainly based on Lambrecht's system of identifiability and activation.

Lambrecht (1994) argued that traditional partitions such as "theme–rheme", "topic–comment", and "topic–focus" overlook a fundamental categorical issue — namely, that information structure is not composed of discrete, segmental sentence constituents. These binary frameworks tend to divide sentences or propositions into rigid components (e.g., theme vs. rheme; topic vs. comment; topic vs. focus). As an alternative, Lambrecht introduced the key notions of presupposition and focus, which he conceptualized as propositional in nature rather than tied to specific syntactic constituents. In addition to these, assertion and topic are also identified as central elements in the structuring of information.

The difference between "meaning" and "information" is essential for the understanding of the relationship between syntactic constituents and information structure. "Meaning" is a semantic concept expressed either by individual words or the relations between words, while information is expressed via propositions. So, the information of a proposition is realized by establishing the relationships between informative units instead of the semantic ones in the proposition. The guideline we resort to must be something information-oriented and not limited by the syntactic configuration or word order of the sentence because these methods are what we should be based on.[①] Lambrecht's "presupposition versus focus" is employed as a vital partition of information structure. In his study, he considered the "old information" to be the pragmatic presupposition, while the "new information" is the pragmatic assertion. His ideas are summarized in general as the following.

(i) Both the presupposition and the new information are "propositional in nature" and the new information generally involves an assertion about a familiar referent, (i.e., the topic).

(ii) The topic is then excluded from the focus (the focal part of the assertion), because (the relevance of) the topic is part of what is presupposed.

(iii) The focus is that part of the assertion that is not presupposed.

(iv) This framework also accommodates the presence of information within an assertion that is neither topical — that is, not what the assertion is about — nor focal. The structure of an assertion can thus be represented as: Assertion = [(TOPIC) (other presupposed material) (FOCUS)]. The topic is typically realized as a syntactic constituent, whereas the focus, though not necessarily a syntactic constituent itself, is usually embedded within one. This syntactic constituent, which generally excludes the topic, is referred to as the focal domain.

In the present study, the above parameters (i.e., presupposition, assertion, focus, topic, identifiability, and activation, whose definitions will be presented in the following sections) are borrowed to explore the configuration of cleft sentences. This study addresses the following questions: First, what is the structural configuration of presupposition, focus, and assertion in cleft sentences? Second, what types of focus structures are exhibited in Chinese cleft constructions? Third, how can the informational components of Chinese

---

[①] This statement does not refute the connection between word order and information structure, as word order serves as a crucial parameter within this domain. However, it is important to emphasize that word order is not the sole determinant of information structure.

clefts — such as focus and topic — be identified and classified in terms of their discourse status?

Key concepts are carefully selected and elaborated upon here to provide a clearer and more comprehensive understanding.

4.1.1.1 Presupposition

Strawson (1964) postulated the condition on which the transmission of information may be realized successfully, named the *Principle of the Presumption of Ignorance*. This principle is to guarantee that information will be delivered successfully only if the information the speaker is trying to convey is not already stored in the hearer's mind. However, considering that the state of ignorance of a hearer is never totally new information added to a zero foundation, this principle must be complemented by another principle, which Strawson calls the *Principle of the Presupposition of Knowledge*.

There are two issues we have to state here, firstly, old information and new information cannot be equated with the old and new referents, and the information of a sentence is not "old information" plus "new information" in a clearly demarcated way. In Lambrecht's terminological practice, he restricted the use of the terms "old information" and "new information" to aspects of information associated with propositions. To avoid confusion, he replaced the "old" and "new" information with "presupposition" and "assertion", which have been mentioned previously. The definitions of presupposition and assertion are given in his book:

"(Pragmatic) presupposition:[①] the set of propositions lexicogrammatical evoked in a sentence that the speaker assumes the hearer already knows or is ready to take for granted at the time the sentence is uttered" (Lambrecht, 1994, p. 52)

Lambrecht (1994) also identified two additional types of presuppositions, the first of which is conscious presupposition. The conscious presupposition is the presupposition evoked by a sentence that concerns the assumed

---

① For the sake of clarity and convenience, the term "pragmatic presupposition" will hereafter to simply as "presupposition".

knowledge state of the addressee. It represents, to some extent, the addresser's judgment or assumption about the state of consciousness or awareness of the addressee at the time of utterance. The other one is called relevance or topicality presupposition. It is the presupposition evoked by a sentence in which the assumptions a speaker has been concerned with the contextual relevance or topicality of a referent in the discourse; that is, the degree to which a referent can be taken to be a center of current interest concerning which a proposition is interpreted as constituting relevant information.

For example, the pragmatic presuppositions lexicogrammatically evoked by the utterance "*I finally met the woman who moved in downstairs*" (1994, p. 51) may be loosely stated as the following set of propositions:

"(i) The addressee can expect and accept the existence of the female individual designated by the definite noun phrase.

(ii) Someone moved in downstairs from the speaker.

(iii) One would have expected the speaker to have met that individual at some earlier point in time.

(iv) The addressee is aware of the referents of the pronouns *I* and *who* at the time these pronouns are uttered.

(v) The proposition expressed by the sentence is construable as relevant information about the referent of *I*; the proposition expressed by the relative clause is construable as relevant information about the referent of *who*. (Lambrecht, 1994, p. 55)"

The first presupposition is evoked by a grammatical morpheme, the definite article *the*; the second is evoked by a grammatical construction, the relative clause *who moved in downstairs*; and the third is evoked by a lexical item, the adverb *finally*. The fourth is the consciousness presupposition. The fifth is the relevance presupposition expressed via the two unaccented pronouns. The five presuppositions are all equally important, however, the last two have no relation to the formal structures. Because the present study is an analysis of information structure based on the syntactic structure of cleft sentences, the consciousness presupposition and the relevance presupposition are not included in the analysis of the present study.

4.1.1.2 Assertion

Together with the pragmatic presupposition, the definition of pragmatic assertion is also postulated by Lambrecht (1994).

"(Pragmatic) assertion: the proposition expressed by a sentence which the hearer is expected to know or take for granted as a result of hearing the sentence uttered." (p. 52)

Thus, unlike presupposition, assertion is a proposition that is established only after the utterance is completed, rather than beforehand. It is established based on presupposition and focus. The assertion is a combination of two sets of propositions — one is the set of the presupposed proposition established before the utterance of the sentence (i.e., presupposition); the other is the non-presupposed proposition which is added to, or superimposed on, the former (i.e., focus). We can formulate the relationship between presupposition, assertion, and focus as "assertion = presupposition + focus".

Lambrecht (1994) stated that because the speaker expects to know something "informative" by hearing a sentence, the assertion must differ from the presupposed set. It is possible, according to Lambrecht (1994), to have a null presupposition instead of a null assertion. For example, in the sentence-focus structures proposed by Lambrecht (1994), there is no presupposition, and the assertion coincides with the focus of the sentence.

4.1.1.3 Focus

Traditionally, the focus is considered to be the complement of the topic. All sentences convey new information, so all sentences must have a focus; however, not all sentences have a topic (Lambrecht 1994). For this reason, it is not accurate to define "focus" as the complement of the "topic". Just as a topic is included in the presupposition without being identical to it, a focus is part of an assertion without necessarily coinciding with it. Within the framework developed by Lambrecht (1994), the focus of a sentence, or rather, the focus of the proposition is seen as the element of information whereby the presupposition and the assertion differ from each other. The focus is the portion of an assertion that cannot be taken for granted at the time of speech. It is the unpredictable or pragmatically non-recoverable element in an utterance. The focus makes an utterance into an assertion.

Previous definitions of "focus" are given by scholars like Bolinger (1954), Halliday (1967), and Jackendoff (1972). Lambrecht's concept of presupposition is pragmatics-oriented, thus making a subtle difference between the two "presuppositions", as does the term "focus". The "presupposition" in the Chomsky-Jackendoff tradition is only one particular subtype of pragmatic presupposition, and the accent rules proposed by these authors are insufficient to account for the focus-presupposition relation in general, for to explain the focus and presupposition only from the perspective of prosody ignores the distinction between focus and activation. Just as Lambrecht (1994, p. 270) stated: "The absence of pitch prominence on a clause or portion of a clause merely has the effect of marking a propositional denotatum as *active*."

Prosodic factors serve as crucial parameters in conveying information structure in both English and Chinese, a fact that is indisputable. However, the present study does not undertake a detailed analysis of prosodic factors for the following two reasons. Firstly, cleft sentences are marked syntactic constructions that fulfill specific pragmatic functions through their unique structural arrangement and configuration. As a result, prosodic factors play a less significant role compared to syntactic mechanisms in conveying their intended meaning. In spoken communication, following the *Principle of Least Effort*,[①] speakers tend to prefer prosodic strategies over syntactic constructions to convey intended meanings, as prosodic prominence

---

[①] Zipf (1949) first proposed the Principle of Least Effort (and the Principle of Sufficient Effort) which is followed by wide discussions. The principle is an overarching principle not only for languages but also everything else in the human universe. Zip (1949, p. 20ff) acknowledged two basic and competing forces—the force of unification (i.e. Speaker's Economy) and the Force of Diversification (i.e. Auditor's Economy). Based on the Principle of Least Effort, many principles for different linguistic branches are proposed, for example, the maxims of conversation (Grice, 1975).

is inherently more economical than syntactically marked structures. Consequently, the functional structures, such as cleft sentences, examined in this study are primarily based on written language.

Furthermore, due to this very reason, all data analyzed in the present study are drawn from a written corpus, thereby excluding prosodic factors from consideration.

Returning to the definition of "focus," it has been established that focus is not merely a complement to the topic, which suggests that the segmentation-based approach is inadequate for defining focus. Both topic and focus belong to the pragmatic category, highlighting their functional roles in discourse rather than their structural segmentation. Lambrecht (1994, p. 207) made one example to illustrate the nature of "focus".

(4-3)   Q: Where did you go last night?
        A: I went to the **movies**.

The expression "the movies" is absolutely informative, being an element of the proposition made up by the entire sentence. However, the new information of the sentence is not the constituent "the movies" or its designatum, but "its role as the second argument of the predicate 'go-to' in the pragmatically presupposed open proposition 'speaker went to x'" (Lambrecht, 1994, pp. 209-210).

Lambrecht (1994) gave his definition of focus as "the semantic component of a pragmatically structured proposition whereby the assertion differs from the presupposition" (p. 213).

In summary, the key characteristics of focus can be outlined as follows.

(i) The focus is an element of a pragmatically structured proposition that makes the utterance of the sentence into an expression of information.

(ii) It is the remaining part when all the presupposed components are taken from an assertion.

(iii) Sometimes, focus coincides with assertion, supposing that there is no presupposition evoked in the sentence.

(iv) The relation between the focus and the proposition is assumed to be unpredictable or non-recoverable for the addressee at the time of the utterance. The focus relation creates a new state of information (assertion) in the mind of the addressee.

(v) The focus of a proposition may be marked prosodically, morphologically, syntactically, or via a combination of the above methods.

4.1.1.4 Topic

The notion of the topic provided by Lambrecht (1994) is different from that proposed by systemic functional linguists. In Lambrecht's study, there is one important feature of the topic that distinguishes it from the views of linguists mentioned above — the topic is no longer the "element which comes first in a sentence", which is the idea proposed by systemic functional linguistics. In English, the sentence-initial position can be taken by either topic or focus, so it cannot be treated as one of the criteria for either of the two terms. Contrarily, the notion of topic/theme as the first element in the sentence is extensively discussed in Prague School research (cf. Firbas, 1966; Fries, 1983; Halliday, 1967).

The topic has sometimes been defined as a "scene-setting" expression, or as an element that sets "a spatial, temporal or individual framework within which the main predication holds" (Chafe, 1976). There are three properties of the topic.

(i) It must have a referent.

(ii) The referent must be identifiable.

(iii) It has a certain degree of pragmatic salience in the discourse.

To define topic within the framework of pragmatic concepts such as amount of information and relevance, Lambrecht (1994) argued that relying solely on syntactic structure to determine topic is neither appropriate nor accurate. To determine whether an entity is a topic in a sentence or not, it is often necessary to take into account the discourse context in which the sentence is embedded. This means "being a discoursal referent" is a criterion of being a topic. Lambrecht (1994) example is explained here:

Speaker A has dialed the wrong number and is asking to speak to a person unknown to speaker B, who receives the phone call.

(4-4)   A: Is Alice there?
       B: There is no Alice here.
       b: ?Alice isn't here.
       c: ? She isn't here.
       d: ? No.

Although "Alice" is a referring expression, it cannot function as the topic for B (i.e., the hearer) because it does not correspond to a specific discourse referent in B's mental representation. A's utterance introduces a presupposition regarding the existence of a woman named Alice, which becomes active in B's mind. However, B is unable to identify the specific Alice that A is referring to (in other words, the referent of "Alice" is not actively evoked in B's cognition).

Under these circumstances, "Alice" cannot occupy the sentence-initial topic position. Instead, the noun phrase (NP) "Alice" must appear in the postverbal focus position.

4.1.2 The connections between these concepts

To demonstrate the relationship between presupposition, assertion, and focus, we will examine two examples of cleft sentences in both English and Chinese. From the perspective of focus structure (as discussed in the following section), both examples belong to the same type, specifically the argument-focus structure.

(4-5)   It is **a watch** that Susan gave Mike.
       Presupposition: Susan gave Mike something(X).
       Focus: a watch
       Assertion: X=a watch

(4-6) 是小明打破窗户的。
Shì Xiǎomíng dǎpò chuānghu de.
SHI$_{aux}$ Xiaoming break window DE$_{ptcl}$.
It is **Xiaoming** who broke the window.
Presupposition: There is someone (X) who broke the window.
Focus: Xiaoming
Assertion:X=Xiaoming

Presupposition, when present, always takes the form of a proposition. While the focus constituent is often a referent, it can sometimes extend beyond that scope (though this is not evident in the previous two examples). Assertion, in turn, serves to establish the relationship between presupposition and focus, linking the given and new information within an utterance. "X" in (4-5) and (4-6) is added by the hearer automatically and intuitively after the sentence is uttered.

4.2 Focus Types and the Configuration of the Information Structure

As Dik (1980, 1997) emphasized, languages not only employ different strategies for information packaging, but also convey varied focus meanings, often referred to as "focus types". The division of focus types is a long-lasting subject being discussed by scholars. It is assumed that there is a bipartition of the types of focus structure (see Halliday, 1967; Kiss, 1998; Rochemont, 1986; Selkirk, 2002, etc.). The difference between the two types lies in the fact that one of the two types aims to provide new information, and the other aims to establish a contrastive relationship by highlighting the focus. Although the distinction between these two types has long been widely recognized in linguistic literature (cf. Halliday, 1967; Rochemont, 1986), scholars have proposed different terms to describe them.For instance,

Kiss (1998) differentiates between identificational focus and information focus, while Gundel distinguishes information focus from contrastive focus. Similarly, Selkirk (2002) categorizes focus into contrastive focus and presentational focus. However, to conduct detailed research on the relationship between the syntactic representation and the focusing functions of the sentence, I'd like to follow some semantic-syntactic based criteria of the focus types. In this regard, I draw upon the criteria proposed by Lambrecht (1994).[①]

Lambrecht claimed the advantage of his criteria in the following way:

"In combining the semantic-syntactic terms "predicate", "argument", and "sentence" with the pragmatic term "focus", my intention is to capture the correlation between certain formal and semantic categories and certain types of communicative functions, such as the function of commenting on a given topic of conversation (predicate focus), of identifying a referent (argument focus), or of reporting an event or presenting a new discourse referent (sentence focus). There is thus a correlation between types of focus structure and type of communicative situation." (Lambrecht, 1994, p. 222)

Lambrecht (1994) identifies three types of focus structure: predicate-focus structure, argument-focus structure, and sentence-focus structure. The communicative functions of these structures have been summarized by Zhou (2008) in Table 4-1.

Table 4-1 Focus classifications and their communicative functions

Focus classifications		Communicative functions
Narrow focus	Argument-focus	Identifying referents, correcting and contrasting
Broad focus	Predicate-focus	Commenting on a topic
	Sentence-focus	Reporting events of presenting referents

[①] Lambrecht's criteria for focus structure types provide a comprehensive classification applicable to various sentence structures, rather than being exclusively designed for cleft sentences.

4.2.1 Predicate–focus structure

The predicate-focus[①] structure is also called the "topic-comment" structure with the focus being the predicate of the sentence (i.e., normally, the sentence constituents other than the subject). In the present study, "shi" copula sentences are treated as of this type. The information structure of the predicate-focus structure is shown by this example from Lambrecht (1994, p. 226).

(4-7) Sentence: My car **broke down**.
Presupposition: "speaker's car is a topic for comment x"
Assertion: "x=broke down"
Focus: "broke down"
Focus domain: VP

The focus domain is the smallest constituent that contains the focus, and in this sentence, the focus domain is a VP. The function of the sentence is to provide the nonpresupposed information as a complement to the subject (i.e., something that happened to the speaker's car).

In the present study, "shi" copula sentences pose challenges in distinguishing genuine cleft sentences, as their superficial structural similarities can lead to ambiguity in classification. However, from the perspective of information structure, "shi" copula sentences are predicate-focus structures with the focus falling on the predicate (the whole predicate, not any part of it) of the sentence. The function of the "shi" copula sentence is to provide more information about the subject from the perspectives of identities, classifications, attributions, or other explanations, to take one example.

[①] Predicate here is a semantic concept with its counterpart being the argument. It refers to the event or state the sentence is dealing with; while arguments are the things that refer to the participants in the event/state. Typically, predicates are expressed by verbs. In Chinese, there are nominal predicates and adjective predicates.

(4-8) 我是种田的。
　　　Wǒ shì zhòngtián de.
　　　1SG SHI$_{cop}$ farm DE$_{nomi}$.
　　　I am a farmer.
　　　Presupposition: " 'I' is the topic of comment x".

"SHI$_{cop}$" is incorporated within the focus domain of the sentence, functioning as a copula predicate.

　　　Focus: X= (am a farmer)
　　　Focus domain: VP
　　　Assertion: I am a farmer

The focus following the copula "shi" conveys no contrastive and exhaustive information. The focus, semantically, is the predicate of the sentence. Out of context, the predicate can be any constituent expressing attribution, classification, etc., and there is no exhaustive focus expressed by the predicate-focus structure, so "shi" copula sentences in Chinese are predicate-focus structures.

4.2.2　Argument–focus structure

In the argument-focus structure, the focus identifies the missing argument in a presupposed open proposition. The focal argument in an argument-focus structure is usually, but not necessarily, the subject of the sentence. The function of the argument-focus structure is to make the argument the focus by prosodic, syntactic, or any other means. Unlike the other two types, the specificational function of the focus constituent in the argument-focus structure (i.e., argument), to some extent, leads to the exhaustivity of the focus.

(4-9)　Sentence: **My car** broke down.
　　　Presupposition: "something (=X) broke down"

Assertion: "X=my car"

Focus: "my car"

Focus domain: NP

The sentence can be considered as a means of correction by narrowing the focus domain in the following scenario.

(4-10) A: I heard that your motorcycle broke down.

B: No, **my car** broke down.

Lambrecht (2001) put forward that cleft formation is a formal strategy for expressing argument focus. To put it in a cleft sentence, the unmarked form of argument (4-9) sentence can be changed into.

(4-11) It is **my car** that broke down.

Due to the particularities of the syntactic configuration of English cleft sentences, scholars (e.g., Lambrecht, 2000) considered the argument-focus structure as the major focus group of English cleft sentences. However, by observing their Chinese counterparts, it is easy to find out that the argument-focus structure is not the only type of focus structure they express, instead, adjunct-focus structures are also accepted in Chinese cleft sentences.

4.2.3 Sentence–focus structure

There is one prominent characteristic of the sentence-focus structure — the pragmatic presupposition does not exist in its information structure. In other words, assertion and focus coincide in these structures. The function of this type of sentence is to give rise to the eventive or confirmative interpretation of the proposition.

(4-12)　Sentence: **My car**[①] **broke down**.
　　　　Presupposition: null
　　　　Assertion: "speaker's car broke down"
　　　　Focus: "speaker's car broke down"
　　　　Focus domain: Sentence

The focus domain of this type is the whole sentence.

In the present study, some of the superficially similar "shi" sentences are the sentence-focus structure without any assignment of presupposition. Based on the criteria proposed by Hole (2011), Büring and Križ (2013), and others, and in light of the subtle distinctions between the Chinese "shi...de" cleft construction and cleft-like "shi" sentences, this study adopts the criteria for cleft sentences outlined in Chapter 5. Constructions that do not satisfy these criteria are excluded from the selection procedure.

4.2.4　Types of focus structure of Chinese cleft sentences

The classification criteria for focus types proposed by Lambrecht (1994) are adopted in this study, as they align well with the structure of Chinese sentences. Corresponding sentence patterns for each focus type are identified and exemplified in the present analysis. In Chinese cleft sentences, while the argument-focus structure is indeed one of the possible types, other non-argument focus structures also exist. However, the semantic distinctions between "argument" and "predicate" alone are insufficient for categorizing focus types in the present study.

(4-13)　我是**昨天到北京**的。
　　　　Wǒ shì zuótiān dào Běijīng de.

[①] Interestingly, scholars such as Lambrecht find that in both argument-focus structure and sentence-focus structure in English, the prosodic prominence of the sentence falls on the argument of the sentence. However, the unmarked position of prosodic prominence of an unmarked English sentence should be the final position in the sentence.

1SG SHI$_{aux}$ yesterday arrive Beijing DE$_{ptcl}$.

It was **yesterday** when I arrived in Beijing.

Presupposition: I arrived in Beijing.

Focus: yesterday

Focus domain: NP

The focus, as an adjunct of the sentence, is inserted into the presupposition " I arrived in Beijing" which is a canonical sentence before the insertion. The focus "yesterday" is neither the argument nor the predicate of the sentence. Being the smallest constituent that contains the focus, another type of focus domain has to be established for this kind of structure. Because the focus is an adjunct of the sentence, in this present study, structures like this are considered to be adjunct focus structures.

The types of focus structures in Chinese cleft sentences in actual use are investigated in the present study through the corpus search and the subsequent analysis.

4.3 Identifiability, Referentiality, and Definiteness

4.3.1 Referentiality and identifiability

Referentiality and identifiability are concepts in linguistics that refer to how entities or referents are identified and referred to in language. They are closely related and often used interchangeably, but they have slightly different nuances.

Referentiality refers to the ability of language to refer to or denote entities or referents in the world. In other words, it is the property of a linguistic expression to have a referent in the *external reality*. For example, in the sentence "I saw a dog in the park", the word "dog" is referential because it refers to a specific entity in the world, i.e., a dog.

Identifiability, on the other hand, refers to the extent to which a referent is identifiable or known to the listener or reader based on the *linguistic context*. It is a pragmatic aspect of reference that depends on the shared knowledge, context, and discourse situation between the speaker/writer and the listener/reader. A referent can be identifiable if it is known or can be easily inferred from the context, or non-identifiable if it is unknown or cannot be inferred from the context.

Languages may use various linguistic strategies to indicate referentiality. For example, in English, definite articles (i.e., "the") are often used to refer to identifiable entities, whereas indefinite articles (i.e., "a" or "an") are used for non-identifiable entities. In some languages, word order or verb inflections may also convey information about referentiality and identifiability.

In some cases, referentiality and identifiability can be context-dependent and subject to interpretation. For example, a pronoun like "it" or "he" may refer to a specific entity in one context but be ambiguous or non-referential in another context without additional information.

Referentiality and identifiability are important concepts in the study of language and discourse, as they play a crucial role in how entities are referred to, identified, and understood in communication.

4.3.2 Identifiability and definiteness

There is more than one way to realize the identifiability of a referent in a discourse. Identifiability is a *cognitive* and *pragmatic* concept, while definiteness is a *grammatical* one. Definiteness is one of the ways to realize identifiability. As Lambrecht put it, "the grammatical category of definiteness is a formal feature associated with nominal expressions which signal whether or not the referent of a phrase is assumed by the speaker to be identifiable to the addressee. (Lambrecht, 1994, p.79).

Identifiability involves the speaker's assumptions about whether the addressee can mentally identify a referred entity in a given context. A referent is classified as identifiable if the speaker believes that, based on the linguistic description of the noun phrase and the context, the addressee can differentiate the specific entity from others of the same or different categories. If the addressee cannot do so, the referent is considered nonidentifiable. And the speaker's choice of language forms reflects firstly, his/her assumption about the hearer's state of mind and; secondly, his or her purpose of the utterance (i.e., denoting some referents or making a general description, etc.). To make two examples to illustrate.

(4-14) Anna is afraid of *the dog*.
(4-15) Anna is afraid of *a dog*.

By using "the dog" in (4-14), the speaker assumes that the hearer is in a position to identify which particular dog Anna is afraid of. And this confirmative assumption may be perceived by the knowledge background shared by the speaker and the hearer or it may be triggered by some situational context of that utterance, etc. On the other hand, in the sentence (4-15), the speaker assumes that the hearer is not in a position to identify which particular dog Anna is afraid of, or traced back to the purpose of the sentence (4-15), the speaker's purpose by uttering this sentence is not to denoting the particular dog by showing its specificity and uniqueness, but to express the general fact that — Anna is afraid of the animal dog in general.

Concepts of identifiability has been introduced by various names in the literature such as old vs. new (Halliday, 1967), given vs. new (Clark, 1977), definite vs. indefinite (Chafe, 1976; Lyons, 1977), and uniquely identifiable vs. nonidentifiable (Gundel et al, 1993). Despite some differences in terminology and meaning among authors, this article adopts the definitions of identifiable and nonidentifiable as outlined by Lambrecht (1994), without delving into the details of these differences. And this section will further discuss the differences between identifiability and definiteness.

In this article, the term "definiteness" is being used as a grammatical concept to encode identifiable and nonidentifiable referents. This encoding is achieved through phonological, morphological, and positional devices. Whether definiteness is considered a grammatical category in a specific language depends on how it is defined. Definiteness can be understood in a broad sense, which characterizes identifiable expressions universally disregarding language differences. The universal devices for definiteness include pronouns, proper names, and definite noun phrases. However, in the current literature, definiteness is usually understood in a narrow sense — the defining criteria are whether there exists an independent linguistic form whose primary function is to indicate identifiability and whether the features of definiteness and indefiniteness are mandatory and unique to nominal expressions in the language.

Languages such as English and French typically indicate definiteness through articles and bound morphemes, such as affixes, which are collectively referred to as simple definites, thereby establishing definiteness as a grammatical category. However, in languages such as Chinese, Japanese, Czech, Russian, Warlpiri, Lango, Hindi, and Indonesian, identifiability is primarily indicated by complex definites such as proper names, demonstratives, personal pronouns, and possessives, as well as other grammatical means such as word order. Complex definites encode several grammatical features like deixis, person, saliency, topicality, and identifiability all at once. The key difference between simple definites and complex definites is that the encoding devices in the former have undergone grammaticalization to indicate identifiability or non-identifiability, while the latter encodes multiple grammatical features simultaneously.

Chen (2004) stated that the grammatical category for the narrow "definiteness" –article in Chinese is not fully developed. The terms "definite" and "indefinite" are commonly used in literature to refer to two groups of formal expressions that may or may not be identifiable, along with other grammatical and pragmatic attributes.

The mapping between the categories of definite and indefinite is not always clear-cut. For instance, the interpretation of an indefinite expression as specific or non-specific depends on the context. Let's check the relationship between indefinite expression and specificity through the following example borrowed from Iemmolo and Arcodia (2014).

(4-16)　I am looking for *a book*.

"A book" can be explained as specific or non-specific depending on the actual state of the speaker — whether the speaker is looking for a particular book or not. This ambiguity is resolved through anaphoric reference in discourse. If the referent is specific, a definite anaphoric expression must be used, whereas if the referent is non-specific, an indefinite pronoun or NP is necessary. Similarly, generic NPs, which refer to an entire class of entities or a representative set of its members, are considered identifiable.

In languages such as English, definiteness is regularly expressed by the grammatical category of articles. However, in languages without articles, definiteness is marked by other grammatical means, such as word order, case-marking particles, or numeral classifiers.

Chen (2004) made elaborate studies of the definiteness of Chinese. He proposed that besides the identifiable referring expressions such as personal nouns, proper nouns, there are some definiteness-inclined expressions in Chinese, however, definiteness is still on the path of grammaticalization.

As is discussed in more detail later, noun phrases (NPs) in Chinese fall into three major formal categories in terms of how the pragmatic property of identifiability is encoded: definite, indefinite, and indeterminate (cf. Chen, 2004).

Although there are no articles in Chinese, demonstratives are developing the uses of a definite article, and yi "one+classifier" has developed the uses of an indefinite article and the indeterminate lexical codings include bare NPs and cardinality expressions (Chen, 2004). The identifiability of the indeterminate expressions is closely related to their positions in the sentence.

In Chinese, indefinite/definite nouns are typically formed using various methods such as using classifiers (also known as measure words), demonstratives, or possessive pronouns. Let's take a closer look at each of these methods:

4.3.2.1 Classifiers

In Chinese, classifiers often come after the numeral and before the noun, and as a whole they can serve as a way to indicate indefiniteness. For example:

(4-17)　一本书 (one book) (using the classifier 本)

(4-18)　两只猫 (two cats) (using the classifier 只)

(4-19)　三张桌子 (three tables) (using the classifier 张)

4.3.2.2 Demonstratives

Demonstratives are usually used to indicate the location or distance of an object in relation to the speaker. They can also be used to indicate definiteness. For example:

(4-20)　这本书 (this book)

(4-21)　那个人 (that person)

(4-22)　这些学生 (these students)

In these examples, "这 (this)" and "那 (that)" are demonstratives that can indicate definiteness by specifying the proximity of the noun to the speaker.

4.3.2.3 Possessive Pronouns

Possessive pronouns are used to indicate ownership or possession of a noun, and they can also convey definiteness. For example:

(4-23)　我的朋友 (my friend)

(4-24)　他们的车 (their car)

In these examples, "我的 (my)" and "他们的 (their)" are possessive pronouns that indicate definiteness by expressing ownership or possession.

It is essential to recognize that Chinese is a context-dependent language, wherein the definiteness of a noun is often inferred from the surrounding linguistic or conversational context. Various linguistic strategies, including classifiers, demonstratives, and possessive pronouns, are frequently employed to indicate definiteness. However, their presence is not always obligatory. The omission of these markers does not inherently signify that a noun is indefinite in Chinese.

4.4 Identifiability and Activation in Discourse

As mentioned before, cognitive statuses of the mental representations of discourse referents and informational constituents are discussed by "identifiability" or "activation".

4.4.1 Identifiability

Identifiability is a cognitive category first proposed by Chafe (1976). He used the term "identifiable" to express the status of the designated referents in the mind of the speaker instead of "known" or "familiar". An identifiable referent is one for which a shared representation already exists in the speaker's and the hearer's mind at the time of utterance, while an unidentifiable referent is one for which a representation exists only in the speaker's mind. The relationship between the identifiable referent and the unidentifiable referent and the relationship between presupposed and asserted propositions are alike. A presupposed proposition is the proposition shared by both the speaker and the hearer through either internal or external knowledge. The difference between presupposed proposition and an identifiable referent is that the latter may not be presupposed to exist; instead, it has a certain representation in the mind of the hearer and the representation can be evoked in a given discourse. For example, in the sentence "The earthquake yesterday caused the big blackout". The presupposed proposition is "There was an earthquake yesterday", and the speaker uses the two identifiable referents ("the earthquake" and "the big blackout") of the sentence to suggest to the hearer, via the form of the expression (definite article in this case), that the speaker assumes that the hearer has some mental representations of the individual and the event designated by those expressions.

Whether a referent is identifiable or not is decided mainly through the following three aspects.

(i) Grammatical factors. Some grammatical factors like articles in languages such as English are the most unmarked way of expressing the identifiability of a referent.

(ii) Discoursal factors. If a referent can be traced back into the previous context, it is identifiable to the speaker but not necessarily to the hearer. In the previous example (4-4), for hearer B, the referent of "Alice" can be traced back to A. So, it is identifiable for B, though it is not necessarily a topic. The identifiability of the topic is varied in degrees in different sentences. Lambrecht (1994) proposed the Topic Acceptability Scale, summarizing the acceptability of the identifiability of the topic (see 4.4.3). Checking the identifiability of the topic in the Chinese cleft sentence is one of the tasks of the present study.

(iii) External factors, Chen (2004) explained that some referents can be inferred from other activities and entities in the discourse through logical reasoning due to general knowledge of the interrelationship between the entities or activities involved. This *shared background information* triggers the mental representation of other activities or entities automatically in the consciousness of the participants during the utterance. It is often captured by the theoretical constructs in cognitive sciences such as "frame" "schema" "script", etc.

Based on these three criteria, there are complicated mechanisms in languages to show the identifiability of a constituent. The detailed methods may differ from language to language. By investigating the identifiability of the information constituents, especially the focus and the topic of the cleft sentence, the study aims to show the mechanism of the identifiability of focus and topic constituents in Chinese cleft sentences.

4.4.2 Activation

With the idea "that our minds contain very large amounts of knowledge or information, and that only a very small amount of this information can be focused on, or be "active" at any one time" (Chafe, 1987, p.22ff), Chafe argued that a particular "concept" may be in any one of three activation states, which he called *active, semi-active* (or *accessible*) and *inactive* respectively. An active concept refers to one that is currently lit up, representing a concept within an individual's conscious focus at a given moment. An accessible/semi-active concept is one "that is in a person's peripheral consciousness, a concept of which a person has a background awareness, but one that is not being directly focused on". An inactive concept is one "that is currently in a person's long-term memory, neither focally nor peripherally active" (chafe, 1987, p.25).

Regarding the degree of accessibility, Huang (2007) explained the different degrees of accessibility by the long- or short-term memory of the hearer as well as the context in which the referents are involved. The entities that are retrieved from encyclopedic knowledge are stored in long-term memory and are represented by low accessibility markers. Entities or activities which are present in the physical surroundings are in the short-term memory and therefore are encoded with intermediate accessibility markers. Entities or activities mentioned in the immediately preceding context are stored in the short-term memory and could be perceived with the highest accessibility.

There are two formal ways to express the active status of a referent: firstly, by a lack of pitch prominence; secondly by the pronominal coding of the relevant linguistic expression. As for the formal expression of the inactive status of a referent, the conditions are the opposite of those of active referents. The semi-activeness is much more complicated than the other two states, which is why it has aroused interest among scholars for so many years. Defining the semi-active discourse referent seems trickier. According to Chafe, semi-active (accessible) referents can be of two kinds. A referent ("concept") may become semi-active either by the deactivation from an earlier state, normally by having been active earlier in the previous discourse, or it can become semi-active because it is one member of the set of expectations associated with a "schema". A schema is defined by Chafe as "a cluster of interrelated expectations (Chafe, 1987, p.29)".

Lambrecht (1994) added another kind of accessible referent. This type of referent is accessible due to its presence in the external world beyond the text. He presumed one scenario: sitting in an office with a friend, one might say "Those pictures sure are ugly" with reference to some photographs on the wall which the speaker assumes his/her addressee can easily access the referent of, although it may be that the hearer cannot do so.

Accessibility (semi-activeness) of a referent can thus be ascribed to three factors: deactivation from an earlier state, inference from a cognitive schema or frame, or presence in the text-external world. The first factor is called "textually accessible" by Lambrecht; the second is "inferentially accessible" and the third is "situationally accessible". The two categories "textually accessible" and "situationally accessible" correspond to the text-internal and text-external world respectively, while the category "inferentially accessible" is neutral concerning this distinction: a referent can be inferred from an element in the linguistic as well as in the extra-linguistic context.

From a strictly grammatical perspective, a binary distinction is justified, which refers to the distinction between referents that are marked as being active (attenuated pronunciation and/or pronominal coding), and those which are not so marked. But this is not to say that the postulation of an intermediary category "accessible" has no grammatical reality. The difference between accessible and inactive referents can have syntactic consequences;

in particular, it can influence the position of a constituent in the sentence or the choice of one rather than another grammatical construction. Different syntactic constraints on the coding of inactive and accessible referents have been observed by Prince (1981) and Chafe (1987), who both concluded that subjects of English are active and accessible referents instead of inactive ones. Semi-activeness does have grammatical realization in Chinese. Chen (2004) treated bare NPs and cardinality expressions as "indeterminate" lexical encodings. This type is neutral in respect of the interpretation of identifiability. So, the identifiability of these expressions is highly decided by other syntactic factors, i.e., the word order of the sentence or the occurrence of their referents in previous discourse, etc.

The relationship between identifiability and activation and other terms involved are illustrated in the following diagram (Figure 4-1) borrowed from Lambrecht (1994).

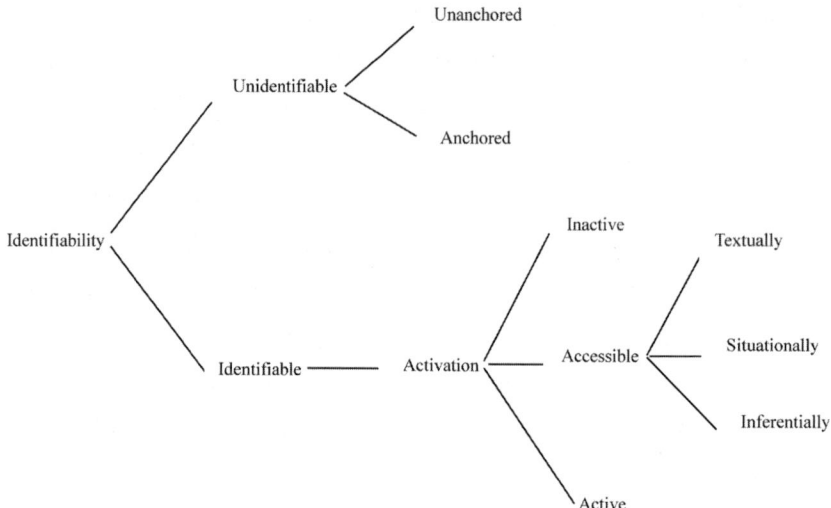

Figure 4-1 Model of Identifiablity (Lambrecht, 1994, p109)

Unidentifiable referents are referents that are represented by brand-new information and do not present in the mind of the hearer by any means. The status of unidentifiable is divided into two subtypes: unanchored and anchored. The anchored referent is the item being part of the previous discourse or part of the situation. For example, the first example below delivers the unanchored unidentifiable referent and the second delivers an anchored one.

(4-25)   I saw *a cat* in the park yesterday.

(4-26)   *A student* I taught before went abroad recently.

The status of activation is divided into three types: inactive, accessible, and active. The status of inactive is called "unused" by Prince (1981) which means the referent is a discourse-new but hearer-old one. For example:

(4-27)   *Your mother* just came.

The identifiable active status of a referent suggests that it is both a piece of discourse-old and hearer-old information which can be evoked by the hearer most easily. Grammatical methods such as pronouns are used to designate the activeness of the referent.

(4-28)   I bought a book yesterday. *It* is one of the best sellers this year.

The subtypes of the accessible category can be explained by the following examples.

4.4.2.1 Textually-accessible

(4-29)   I met one girl and one boy today. They are probably lovers, and the boy started to hit the girl suddenly, but *the girl* just stood there and did nothing to stop him.

The referent "the girl" is grammatically preceded by the definite article "the", which means it is a grammatically identifiable concept. However, instead of being an identifiable active one, it is a textually accessible referent. A textually accessible expression requires an explicit antecedent "which has not been mentioned in the last two or three clauses and is thus only semi-active" (Baumann, 2006, p.157).

4.4.2.2 Situationally-accessible

Situational accessibility means that the referent can be accessed through an extra-textual context. The extra-textual context, for example, could be the spatial-temporal conditions shared by both the speaker and the hearer.

(4-30)   *Those pictures* sure are ugly.

This example is quoted from Lambrecht (1994). When the speaker and the hearer are in the same place at the same time, without particular indication, the hearer would retrieve the referents the speaker refers to.

4.4.2.3 Inferentially-accessible

An inferential accessible referring expression does not have explicit antecedents. They are (semi-)activated by bringing inference (cf. Clark, 1977) from another entity already present in the hearer's discourse model.

(4-31)   A: Are you ok?/ Why do you have a stomachache?/ What happened to you?
B: I bought a combo from KFC, *the ice Coke* made my stomach ache.

The referent represented by the grammatical constituent "the ice Coke" (definite article+NP) does not appear in the previous discourse, and cannot be retrieved situationally. However, anyone who is familiar with fast food combos such as those sold at KFC knows that ice Coke may be included in the combo, so the information is easily accessed by the hearer.

The investigation of the identifiability of the informational constituent (i.e., focus) of Chinese cleft sentences is based on the above criteria proposed by Lambrecht (1994). However, a modified version is proposed in the present study to adjust to the Chinese language based on these criteria. Some ideas from Chen (2004) are borrowed. Chen (2004) summarized that the uses of English definite articles fall into four categories — situational, anaphoric, shared specific or general knowledge, and associative. By using these categories, Chen (2004) also tested the identifiability of referents in languages without articles, such as Chinese.

4.4.3 Identifiability/activation and the topic

Topics are relationally given. "The association of topics with definiteness across languages suggests that topics must be familiar (or at least uniquely identifiable)" (Gundel and Fretheim, 2004, p.181).

Lambrecht (1994, p.165) proposed the *Topic Acceptability Scale* as Figure 4-2.

Figure 4-2 The Topic Acceptability Scale (Lambrecht 1994, p.165)

Acceptability can be, to some extent, tested by the effort consumed by the hearer to retrieve the referent. The cognitive efforts made to interpret the referents increase from an "active" topic to a "brand-new unanchored" topic. The active topic refers to the one with obvious markers such as unaccented pronominals. Accessible topics are the ones that can be retrieved by inferring other logical relationships, so much time is needed for the processing task.

4.4.4 Identifiability/activation and the focus

Unlike a topic, a focused constituent is in principle free concerning the question of identifiability and activation. Although the focus is always treated as the "new" information of a sentence, what causes its "newness" is not the status of its denotatum in the discourse but the newness of its relation to the asserted proposition at the time of utterance. So, it is the new relationship, instead of the new denotatum (or reference). Therefore, focus does not equal "inactiveness"; instead, the status of the identifiability of the focus is context-dependent.

Being a marked structure, the information structure of cleft sentences differs from unmarked ones. One of the differences is reflected in the identifiability of focus constituents. Cowles (2012) stated that focus, particularly when encoded using clefts, appears to increase the identifiability of referents in memory.

In the present study, the discussion of the identifiability of the focus constituent is treated as an important task.

4.5 Cognitive Perspective on Identifiability

Epstein (2002) suggested an alternative approach to dealing with definiteness, one that goes beyond the concept of identifiability. He drew on the works of McCawley (1979, 1985) and Hawkins (1991) and argued that definite descriptions are interpreted based on subsets or domains within the universe of discourse that are pragmatically determined. Therefore, it is not just identifiability that determines the use of articles, but also the dynamic cognitive activity between the speaker and listener within the universe of discourse. After examining the usage of the definite article in various published materials, Epstein (2002) concluded that the main function of the article is to indicate the accessibility of a discourse referent. Specifically, it signals the availability of an access path through a configuration of mental spaces or cognitive domains.

In a general way, the cognitive interpretation of identifiability refers to how the human mind perceives and understands the concept of identifiability in various contexts. Identifiability is often used to describe the degree to which an individual or a specific piece of information can be distinguished or recognized from others. From the perspective of cognition, identifiability can be explained from different angles. Identifiability can also be related to memory and recall processes. When information is easy to remember or recall, it may be considered more identifiable. Identifiability can also be influenced by the context or familiarity of an individual or object. For instance, a person who is well-known in a particular community or social group may be considered more identifiable within that context, but less identifiable in a different context. Identifiability can also be related to how the human mind processes and attends to information. If an individual or object attracts more attention or cognitive processing, it may be considered more identifiable. For example, an object that is highlighted, emphasized, or stands out in a display may be perceived as more identifiable compared to objects that are less prominent or visually obscured.

A classical model showing the relationship between identifiability and human cognition is proposed by Gundel et al. (Figure 4-3). Gundel et al. (1993) suggested that determiners and pronouns limit the potential referents by conventionally indicating distinct cognitive statuses (i.e., memory and attention states) that are believed to exist in the mind of the addressee in relation to the intended referent.

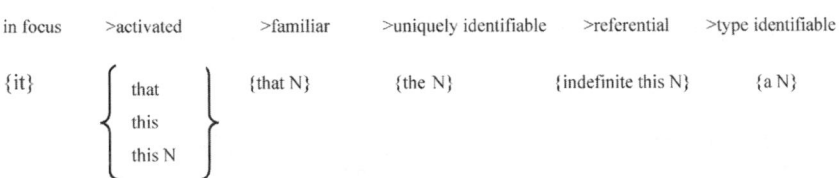

Figure 4-3 The Givenness Hierarchy (Gundel et al, 1993:284)

One way for a speaker to create an identifiable representation is by retrieving an already existing representation from their memory, whether it is stored in their long-term or working memory. This is because anything familiar can be identified as unique by the hearer.

A referent can be recognized as identifiable even if it hasn't been explicitly mentioned in the previous discourse, due to its familiarity from cultural knowledge, general experience, or its presence in the spatiotemporal context of the utterance.

Previous familiarity is one of many ways to meet the criteria for being identifiable. The identifiability of a referent can be encoded by a representation already existing in memory (i.e., through the mechanism of familiarity) or by establishing a new unique representation. By establishing a new unique representation, we mean the hearer makes a unique representation based on the phrases of the current utterance. This is demonstrated in the following example.

(4-32) I've just been to a wedding. *The bride* wore blue. (Lyons, 1999, p.7)

"The bride" does not refer to a particular entity that the hearer can already be expected to have represented in their memory. But they are identifiable since the hearer can establish a unique representation by way of a bridging inference to a recently activated entity. To rephrase, the process of representation involves making a connection between a recently activated entity and a new one through a bridging inference. This connection is often facilitated by a familiar *script* or *frame*, such as the expectation of a bride at a wedding. However, the specific references for the phrases that can be inferred may not be stored in memory at the time the referring phrase is encountered.

4.6 Summary

To establish the relationship between the information structure and the syntactic/semantic form as well as the mental representation of the information constituent, this study borrows some relevant theories of information structure (including types of focus by Lambrecht, etc.), and a new model of identifiability is introduced. Guided by these theories, the following 2 problems are checked and discussed based on the data in the following discussion chapters.

(i) The focus types of cleft sentences in Chinese according to their different focus domains.

(ii) The identifiability of the focus and topic constituents and their grammatical referents.

Chapter 5

Methodology and Data Collection

This study is a qualitative research paying attention to the analysis of the corpus-based data collected from the online Chinese corpora (i.e., CCL and BCC). The CCL Corpus comprises a diverse range of linguistic data, including colloquial speech (e.g., Beijing dialect surveys), materials from films and television programs (such as lectures and works by Stephen Chow), web-based content, and written texts. Among these, newspaper articles constitute the largest proportion. The corpus contains a total of 783,463,175 Chinese characters, of which 581,794,456 are from modern Chinese sources and 201,668,719 from classical Chinese texts.

The BCC Corpus is a large-scale online corpus with a primary focus on the Chinese language. It contains approximately 15 billion words, encompassing a wide range of domains, including newspapers (2 billion), literature (3 billion), microblogs (3 billion), science and technology (3 billion), general discourse (1 billion), and classical Chinese texts (2 billion).

Due to the limitations inherent in the automatic retrieval of corpus data, the majority of the work is conducted manually, meaning that each qualifying sentence is annotated manually. Consequently, a clear and precise delineation of the criteria for manual searching becomes critically important.

In this chapter, the following tasks are fulfilled.

(i) To introduce the main method of the data collection and the choice of corpora and genres.

(ii) To explain how the data are retrieved and the steps of collection and selection.

(iii) To illustrate how the data is being used in the sebsequent two analyses.

5.1 Data Source

The previous literature mainly uses introspective evidence to support the view about cleft sentences in Chinese. This study resorts to the corpus-based method in selecting data from the natural use of the language; and more importantly, the real context is involved in the analysis to guarantee the objectivity. In this study, the online corpora CCL and BCC are used. Besides the searched data from the two corpora, some introspective examples are also used to explain some phenomena. The primary function of the corpora is to provide the empirical data.

The utilization of the corpus adheres to three guiding principles.

Firstly, the corpus size must be maintained at a reasonable scale, ensuring that it is sufficiently large to encompass all relevant data[①] while remaining manageable to facilitate the manual selection process. Given the extensive number of sentences containing similarly structured strings, manually collecting data on an individual basis is impractical. Therefore, specific sections of the corpora are extracted as qualified sub-corpora to facilitate a more efficient secondary selection process. It is important to clarify that, since the primary search is conducted automatically and its results do not constitute the final dataset required for this study, the overall scale of the corpora is not pre-determined. All data obtained from the primary search must undergo manual sorting during the secondary selection process before being finalized as the output of the corpus search procedure. Consequently, the datasets derived from the primary search are more effectively controlled in terms of capacity. Furthermore, the sub-corpora are not merely randomly extracted portions of the original corpora; rather, they are curated subsets

---

① "Relevant data" here is different from the "qualifying data". The former refers to all the data that consist both of the "qualifying" cleft sentences the "nonqualifying" ones with similar syntactic structures. There are two search steps in the search procedure—the primary and the secondary search. All the possible data collected from the primary search will be sorted in the secondary procedure until the remaining ones are all cleft sentences.

representing two distinct text styles.

Secondly, in the present study, a broader genre classification is adopted rather than a fine-grained subcategorization. Informal texts, including data from modern plays and television talk shows, are grouped into a single sub-corpus. In contrast, formal texts comprise essays such as legal documents, newspaper articles, and writings in the social sciences.

Thirdly, to ensure a balanced outcome, it is essential to maintain a comparable scale among the datasets selected from the primary search results. In this study, following the primary search, a random selection of 20,000 sentences is extracted to constitute the datasets designated exclusively for the secondary selection process.

5.2 Data Extraction

The data collection process in the present study comprises two distinct stages: the primary search procedure and the secondary selection procedure. The primary search is the procedure aiming to automatically retrieve data holding structures of the searching strings by the online corpora. The secondary selection process, which must be conducted manually due to the limitations of the automated search, excludes non-qualifying instances based on the criteria for Chinese cleft sentences established in the present study.

5.2.1 Primary search

In the primary search, the following strings are the indexes used in the corpora searching procedure by the POS taggings.

是 $15 的 (shi $15 de) (CCL corpus)

是 * 的 w (BCC corpus)

The wildcard "$15" is the searching language of the CCL corpus representing that there are 15 characters between the two characters "是" and "的". The determination of the 15-characters length is based on relevant surveys about the average length of Chinese simple sentences.

The length of Chinese sentences is studied mainly by scholars from computational linguistics. Their studies aim to innovate software or corpus tools such as corpus parsing. The following two tables (Tables 5-1 and Tables 5-2) suggest that, firstly, generally speaking, sentences with a length of ten Chinese characters over- whelmingly exist in communications; secondly, different genres have different distributions of simple and complex sentences. For a detailed investigation of the basic sentence length in Chinese and sentence lengths across different text types, see Table 5-1 and Table 5-2.

Table 5-1 The distribution of sentence length by Zong et al. (1999)

Length (characters)	1	2	3	4	5	6	7	8	9	10	11-67
Percentage (%)	15.12	8.34	9.28	8.54	7.68	6.78	5.27	5.27	4.78	4.09	24.85

Table 5-2 Distributions of Chinese sentences in different genres by Li et al. (2014)

Genres	Number of passages	Percentage of the genre	Number of sentences (simple/ complex)	Percentage of complex sentences in the passage	The average length of sentences (simple sentence/ complex sentence)
Literature	225	37.25	24799 (10614/14185)	57.20	21.40 (12.00/ 28.40)
News	156	25.83	6773 (2882/3951)	58.30	25.00 (14.30/ 32.70)
Academic Writing	28	4.64	9395 (4387/ 5008)	53.30	28.10 (18.00/ 3.60)
Essays	195	32.28	3169 (1869/ 1300)	41.00	21.00 (12.90/ 32.60)
Total	604	100	44136 (19692/ 24444)	55.40	23.00 (13.73/ 31.10)

Regardless of genre variation, the average length of a Chinese simple sentence typically ranges from 12 to 18 characters. Based on this observation, a distance of 15 characters is adopted in this study as a reasonable threshold between "shi" and "de".

The results of the primary search include all sentences with the strings. There are huge numbers of sentences qualifying the above trings in the primary search procedure.To cite two examples after the primary search, see Figure 5-1 and Figure 5-2.

Figure 5-1 Partial Results from the Primary Retrieval of the Structure " 是 $15 的 " in CCL

Figure 5-2 Partial Results from the Primary Retrieval of Structure " 是 * 的 w" in BCC

Only the first 20,000 sentences extracted from the corpora are included as the dataset for this stage of analysis.

5.2.2 Secondary selection procedure

The secondary selection procedure is designed to refine the data obtained from the primary search, ensuring the identification of genuine cleft sentences while filtering out those that do not meet the criteria.

The criteria used in the secondary selection procedure are for the exclusion of non-cleft "shi … de" data from the primary search.

Based on the functional and semantic observation of the data collected from the primary search, the criteria applied to the secondary selection procedure are the following two aspects

(i) The sentence exhibits a bipartite structure distinguishing presupposition from focus. In most cases, the presupposition constitutes a proposition, while the focus is a constituent embedded within this presupposition. The removal of the focus constituent does not render the sentence ungrammatical or syntactically and semantically incomplete. The boundary between the "presupposition" and "focus" is not clearly demarcated. " Shi" and "de" cannot be obligatorily assigned to either the "presupposition" or the "focus".

(ii) The focus should be exhaustive. The tests of exhaustivity are summarized in chapter 3.

Any sentence not meeting any of the above properties is excluded from the set of cleft sentences. In the next section, the two criteria are explained, and how the non-cleft "shi … de" sentences were excluded is discussed with examples.

5.3 Criteria for Data Selection and Analysis

This section further explains how these criteria serve as defining characteristics of Chinese cleft sentences. Examples are provided to illustrate the distinctions between cleft and non-cleft sentences based on the four identified aspects.

5.3.1 The distribution of "presupposition" and "focus"

Most sentences have a focus and a presupposition; however, the distribution of presupposition and focus varies in different types of sentences. Considering the distribution of "presupposition" and "focus", it is necessary to talk about the types of focus structures proposed by Lambrecht (1994) first.

According to Lambrecht (1994), focus types are divided into predicate focus structure, argument focus structure, and sentence focus structure due to the different focus domains.① Let us start with the predicate focus structure in Chinese.

I. Predicate focus structure

(5-1)　　A: 你的脚怎么了?

　　　　　　Nǐ de jiǎo zěnme le^2?

　　　　　　2SG DE$_{poss}$ foot how LE$_{aspc}$?　　What happened to your foot?

　　　　　B: 我的脚扭了。

　　　　　　Wǒ de jiǎo niǔ le.

　　　　　　1SG DE$_{poss}$ foot sprained LE$_{aspc}$.

　　　　　　My foot **was sprained**.

　　　　　Presupposition: " speaker's foot is a topic for comment x"

　　　　　Focus: x (was sprained).

　　　　　Assertion: speaker's foot was sprained.

---

① By focus domain, it meant the syntactic domain in a sentence expressing the focus component of the pragmatically structured proposition. (Lambrecht, 1994, p. 214)

Focus domain: VP

The relationship between the presupposition and focus in a predicate focus structure is "topic-comment". In this sentence, the presupposition coincides with the topic, and the presupposition and focus are partitioned into two parts. The function of the sentence is to provide new information about the topic. If we represent presupposition as "P" and focus as "F", then the whole proposition of the sentence is configured as "P+F".

II. Argument focus structure

(5-2) A: 听老李说你的脖子扭到了。
Tīng lǎo Lǐ shuō nǐ de bózi niǔdào le.
Hear Lao-Li say 2SG DE$_{poss}$ neck sprain LE$_{aspc}$.
I heard from Lao Li that you sprained your neck.

B: 不,是我脚踝扭到了。
Bù, shì wǒ jiǎohuái niǔdào le.
Neg, SHI$_{aux}$ 1SG ankle hurt LE$_{aspc}$.
No, it was **my ankle** that got hurt.

Presupposition: "x" sprained.

Focus: my ankle

Assertion: it was may ankle that got hurt.

Focus domain: NP

Again, representing the presupposition as "P" and the focus as "F", the proposition can be formulated as the structure "$P_i + F + P_i$". In this configuration, the presupposition is segmented by the insertion of the focal element. Crucially, the presupposition constitutes a complete proposition prior to the insertion of the focus; that is, even in the absence of the focal element, the presupposition independently remains semantically coherent and felicitous. This structural pattern exemplifies the canonical informational configuration of cleft sentences in both English and Chinese.

III. Sentence-focus structure

(5-3)　A：你今天怎么迟到了？
　　　　Nǐ jīntiān zěnme chídào le?
　　　　2SG today how late LE$_{aspc}$?
　　　　Why are you late today?
　　　　B：我的脚扭了。
　　　　Wǒ de jiǎo niǔ le.
　　　　1SG DE$_{poss}$ foot sprained LE$_{aspc}$.
　　　　My foot was sprained.
　　　　Presupposition: null
　　　　Focus：my foot was sprained.
　　　　Assertion: my foot was sprained
　　　　Focus domain：sentence

The sentence focus structure is called an "event-reporting" structure by Lambrecht (1994). The primary function is to report an event by providing the new information based on no "presupposition", while the focus extends over both the subject and the predicate. Therefore, from the perspective of information structure partitioning, a sentence-focus structure does not exhibit the typical bipartite division into "presupposition" and "focus", since the necessary condition for such a bipartition — namely, the presence of a presupposition — is absent. Similarly, the "shi" emphatic sentence, emphasizing the truth value or the modality of the whole sentence, is a type of sentence-focus structure with a null presupposition. This is the other difference between "shi" emphatic and cleft sentences in Chinese.

(5-4)　这的确是我的问题，我是该为这事儿负责任的。
　　　　Zhè díquè shì wǒ de wèntí, wǒ shì gāi wèi zhè shìr fù zérèn de.
　　　　DEM indeed SHI$_{cop}$ 1SG D$_{eposs}$ problem, 1SG SHI$_{aux}$ should for DEM matter take responsibility DE$_{ptcl}$.

It is indeed my fault; I sure **should take responsibility for this matter**.

In shi-emphatic constructions, the proposition — derived by omitting "shi" and "de" — is emphasized with respect to either its truth value or modal interpretation. In the sentence (5-4), the insertion of the auxiliary "shi" confirms the subjective opinion of the speaker towards the proposition that "I am the person who should be responsible for this problem". The focus is the whole proposition "I should take responsibility for this", and there is no presupposition. However, in cleft sentences, there must be a presupposition that makes the propositional limitation for the exhaustive focus.

It should be noted that Lambrecht's classification of focus structures is adopted here primarily as a general framework for describing the configuration between presupposition and focus. However, given cross-linguistic differences, the specific types of focus in Chinese cleft constructions identified in this study are established based on empirical evidence derived from the collected data. A comprehensive discussion of these focus types is presented in Chapter 6.

Despite the existence of various types of focus structures, it is important to highlight that the relationship between presupposition and focus within the argument-focus structure represents a prototypical configuration shared by both English and Chinese. In cleft constructions, the presupposition functions as a self-contained proposition, whereas the focus introduces information — typically new or contextually emphasized — that elaborates upon or specifies aspects of the presupposition. Crucially, removing the focal element does not render the sentence structurally incomplete. The defining characteristics of the presupposition-focus configuration in Chinese cleft sentences can be summarized in terms of the following aspects.

5.3.1.1 Non–demarcated partition between the presupposition and the focus

A predicate-focus sentence expresses a "topic-comment" relationship between the subject and the predicate, and, in Chinese copula sentences, the presupposition very often coincides with the topic of the sentence, while the focus represents the comment. Thus, in predicate-focus sentences, the boundary between presupposition and focus is distinctly demarcated, and the presupposition by itself does not constitute a complete proposition. Consider the following example of a sentence containing the copula "shi".

(5-5)   他是小学生。
Tā shì xiǎoxuéshēng.
3SG SHI$_{cop}$ pupil.
He is a pupil.
Presupposition: "he" is the topic of comment "x"
Focus: x (is a pupil)
Assertion: He is a pupil.

The above assertion shows "the establishment of an aboutness relation between the topic referent and the event denoted by the predicate" (Lambrecht, 1994, p.226). The topic, as well as the presupposition of the sentence, is the subject " he," and the focus is the copula predicate "is a pupil" with the copula being part of the verbal predicate. The assertion shows the relationship established between the pre- supposition and the focus. The following table shows the relationship (see Table 5-3).

Table 5-3 Information structure of the sentence (5-5)

Predicate-focus sentence	他 He	是小学生 SHI$_{cop}$ a pupil.
	presupposition	focus
	Assertion	

The boundary between presupposition and focus of sentence (5-5) is clearly demarcated. Now let us have a look at the configuration of presupposition and focus in the argument- focus cleft sentence (see Table 5-4).

(5-6) 是**我**打破窗户的。

Shì wǒ dǎpò chuānghù de.

SHI$_{aux}$ 1SG break window DE$_{ptcl}$.

It was **me** who broke the window.

Presupposition: "x" broke the window

Focus: x=me

Assertion: It was me who broke the window

Table 5-4 Information structure of sentences (5-6)

	是 (SHI$_{aux}$)	我 (I)	打破窗户 (broke the window)	的 (DE$_{ptcl}$).
Argument-focus cleft sentence	–	Focus	–	–
		Presupposition (There is somebody who (X) broke the window)		
	Assertion			

The presupposition of the sentence presents the existing fact that "there is someone who broke the window".

The presupposition of the argument-focus structure is much like an existential presupposition proposed by Huang (2014). For example, the presupposition is not " broke the window" instead of the proposition that "there is someone who broke the window", and by providing the focus as "me", the assertion is formed as "there is someone who broke the window, and that person is me" . The predicate "broke the window" is only part of the presupposition.

5.3.1.2 Exclusion of "shi" or "de" from the presupposition and the focus

The verb "shi" functions as an auxiliary verb in the sentence, while "de" serves as a particle. As purely functional elements, they do not independently attach to any specific constituent. Consequently, unlike in a copular sentence, they are not necessarily involved in the presupposition and focus structure of the sentence. For example (see Table 5-5) .

(5-7) 我是昨天到北京的。

Wǒ shì zuótiān dào Běijīng de.

1SG$_{aux}$ yesterday arrive Beijing DE$_{ptcl}$.

It was **yesterday** that I arrived in Beijing.

Table 5-5 Information structure of the sentence (5-7)

我 I	是 SHI$_{aux}$	昨天 yesterday	到北京 arrive Beijing	的 DE$_{ptcl}$
presupposition$_i$	–	focus	presupposition$_i$	–
Assertion	–	–	–	–

This criterion distinguishes cleft sentences from "shi" copula sentences in which "shi" acts as the copula verb and "de" is the nominalizer, relative pronoun, or modifier marker.

(5-8) 我是种田的。

Wǒ shì zhòngtián de.

1SG SHI$_{cop}$ farm DE$_{nomi}$.

I am a farmer.

(5-9) 花是红色的。

Huā shì hóngsè de.

Flower SHI$_{cop}$ red DE$_{modi}$.

The flower **is red**.

In both examples, the presuppositions are the topics of the sentence — "I" and "flower", respectively, and the copula phrases "am a farmer" and "is red" are the verbal predicates of the subjects. The copula and the nominalizer/modifier "de" are involved in the focus of the sentence.

As shown by the cleft examples in the last section, "shi" and "de" are not necessarily involved in the presupposition or the focus. However, this sub-criterion does not distinguish cleft sentences from emphatic sentences, as shown in the following example.

(5-10) 我是该为这件事负责的。
Wǒ shì gāi wèi zhè jiàn shì fùzé de.
1SG SHI$_{aux}$ should for this CL matter take responsibility DE$_{ptcl}$.
I sure should take responsibility for this matter.

In emphatic sentences, there is no presupposition, and the focus is the whole proposition. "Shi" and "de" are not involved in "focus" or "presupposition", just as in the case of cleft sentences (see Table 5-6).

Table 5-6 Information structure of sentences (5-10)

我 I	是 SHI$_{aux}$	该为这件事负责 should take responsibility for this issue	的。 DE$_{ptcl}$
Focus	–	Focus	–
Assertion	–	–	–

Similar to cleft constructions, in emphatic sentences, neither "shi" nor "de" forms part of the focus constituent.

Being an auxiliary focus marker of cleft sentences, the primary function of "shi" is to put the following constituent in the focused position; and being an ending modal particle, the functions of "de" may enhance the modality of the sentence or expressing the tense/aspect property of the action involved in the sentence under particular context. "Shi" and "de" are not necessarily the components of either presupposition or focus. If they were, their omission would render the sentence ungrammatical. As demonstrated in example (5-8), where "de" functions as a nominalizer for the verb phrase, its omission would result in an ungrammatical structure. Compared to the obligatory nature of "de", "shi" in copular sentences is not as strictly bound to the focus constituent. This is because nominal predicates (e.g., "farmer") are grammatically acceptable in Chinese copular constructions.

The concept of nominal predicates was first introduced by Chao (1968). Chinese linguists, including Chao (1968), Lü (1980), Teng (1979) have observed that certain nominal expressions can function as predicates when the copula verb "shi" is omitted. Tang (2001) argued that the parametric variation of categorical features across languages such as English, Chinese, and Japanese is reflected in the structural differences between small clauses in Chinese and English. This variation is characterized by what he terms "bareness"[①], referring to the absence of overt functional elements in certain constructions. Unlike Chao (1968) and Hashimoto (1969), who proposed that nominal predicate sentences in Chinese result from the omission of the copula "shi", Tang (2001) contended that the dual categorical nature of nouns, encompassing both substantive [N] and predicative [V] features, is subject to parametric variation. Specifically, Chinese nouns exhibit a primary categorical feature [N] and a secondary categorical feature [V], which enables Chinese nominals to function as predicates in bare small clauses (SCs[②])

This phenomenon is exemplified in (5-11), where the omission of the copula "shi" results in "zhongtian de" being interpreted as a nominal predicate. Conversely, when the copula is retained, the predicate remains verbal, conforming to a "copula + nominalized phrase" structure. This distinction highlights the flexibility of nominal predicates in Chinese and their parametric differences from English small clauses.

To establish a unified configurative model of "presupposition" and "focus", "shi" is retained within the focus constituent of shi-copula sentences.

---

① Stowell (1989), Longobardi (1994), Tang (2001), and Li (1998) agreed that bare-NP can be a nominal predicate. However, examples are found against this agreement. Sentence A is a typical "shi"-verb predicate sentence; while sentence B shows ungrammatical nominal predicate converted from A.
  A: 他是人。
   Tā shì rén.
   3SG SHI$_{cop}$ person.
   He is a human being.
  B: * 他人。
   *Tā rén.
   *3SG person.

② Bare SC (small clause): bare SC means there is no functional projection inside the construction. Tang (2001) declared that, unlike English SC, the Chinese SC is structurally "bare", which means there is only the lexical projection in the structure.

This indicates that the focus domain of a copular sentence is the verb phrase (VP), which is headed by the copula "shi".

(5-11) 我种田的。
Wǒ zhòngtián de.
1SG farm DE$_{nomi}$.
I am a farmer.

(5-12) 桌上吃的。
Zhuō shàng chī de.
Table top eat DE$_{nomi}$.
The food on the table.

This discussion illustrates that typically, neither "shi" nor "de" is obligatorily included in the presupposition or the focus in cleft sentences; the same situation happens to "shi" emphatic sentences; in copula sentences, "shi" and "de" (especially the modification "de") has to be included in the focus constituent.

5.3.2 The exhaustivity of the focus

The feature of exhaustivity serves as a key distinguishing factor between cleft sentences and non-cleft "shi...de" constructions, such as "shi" emphatic sentences and copular sentences. Given its role in marking a restricted and exclusive focus, exhaustivity functions as a crucial criterion for differentiating cleft structures from other "shi...de" constructions in Chinese.

To further explain the exhaustivity, let us cite one example from Li (2008, p.750).

(5-13) It's **John** that stole the cookie.

The function of the sentence is to stress that "no one else besides John stole the cookie".

The claim that a non-cleft constituent with a pitch accent in English does not inherently convey exhaustive identification is not solely based on intuition. Rather, this claim is empirically supported by exhaustive identification tests, as outlined in Chapter 3, which provide systematic evidence for distinguishing between cleft and non-cleft structures.

Among the testing methods, Paul and Whitman's (2008) test is the most convenient and practical (i.e., by simply adding one clause to the original sentence). The fundamental idea of the test is that under the condition of exhaustivity, asserting that the property denoted by the presupposition also holds of an entity distinct from the focus of the cleft leads to a contradiction, to quote from his study.

(5-14)　It is **Mary** that I gave the book to.

?　[1]It is Mary that I gave the book to, and it is also John that I gave the book to.

The same situation is for Chinese cleft sentences.

(5-15)　? 是小明打破窗户的, 也是小华打破的.
? Shì Xiǎomíng dǎpò chuānghù de, yě shì Xiǎohuá dǎpò de.
? SHI$_{aux}$ Xiaoming break window DE$_{ptcl}$, also SHI$_{aux}$ Xiaohua break DE$_{ptcl}$.
? It was Xiaoming who broke the window, it was also Xiaohua who did that.

The compound sentence linked by the coordinating conjunction " 也 (and)" is pragmatically unacceptable. If the modified sentence is unacceptable, the original sentence expresses exhaustive meanings or focus.

This approach is used in the present study when excluding the non-qual-

---

[1]　The symbol "?" means the sentence is grammatically accepted but pragmatically anomalous.

ifying sentences.

5.4 Classification and Sorting Procedure

The properties explained in the last section are applied as sorting criteria of the manual procedure. This section demonstrates the data-sorting procedure by examples.

Exhaustivity distinguishes cleft sentences from "shi" copula and "shi" emphatic sentences. "Shi" copula sentences are shown as the predicate-focus structure from the perspective of information structure, with the whole predicate as the focus, which means, the focus is usually the VP of the sentence with the copula "shi" as the head of the VP. However, the predicate focus could be replaced by any other VPs or even NPs/APs, without being limited by any propositional conditions. For example:

(5-16)　小明是高中生。

　　　　Xiǎomíng shì gāozhōngshēng.

　　　　Xiaoming SHI$_{cop}$ secondary school student.

　　　　Xiaoming **is a secondary school student**.

In sentence (5-16), a copula sentence, the focus is not restricted to a verbal predicate, such as the one initiated by a copula in the example, but could be any other type of predicate, for example, the nominal predicate[①] and the adjective predicate.

The following example is a copula-less sentence.

(5-17)　今天星期一。(Tang, 2001)

　　　　Jīntiān xīngqī yī.

[①] Copula-less sentences in Chinese are in the form of "subject + nominal predicate". They "are subject to 'Generalized Anchoring Principle', which requires that every clause be anchored at the interface for LF convergence. To satisfy the principle, clauses may be either tense or focused. It is shown that copula-less sentences in Chinese are subject to focus anchoring." (Tang, 2001).

Today Monday.
Today **is Monday**.

"星期一 (Monday)" is the nominal predicate of the example sentence, being an identifying copula-less sentence. The predicate nominals in the copula-less sentences denote the characteristic and quality of the subject. They can be common nouns, proper nouns, and numerals.

The example (5-16) could be reduced into a copula-less identifying sentence too.

(5-18)　小明（是）高中生。

　　　　Xiǎomíng (shì) gāozhōngshēng.

　　　　Xiaoming (SHI$_{cop}$) secondary school student.

　　　　Xiaoming **is a secondary school student**.

While the function of the sentence is to show the identity of the subject, there is no limitation for the focus (i.e., predicate) of the sentence; the identity of "Xiaoming" could be a secondary school student, an officer, a teacher, etc. Besides demonstrating the identity of the subject, the copula-less sentence could also show the characteristics of the subject, as the following sentence.

(5-19)　小明 92 届的。

　　　　Xiǎomíng 92 jiè de.

　　　　Xiaoming 92 class DE$_{rel}$.

　　　　Xiaoming **is from the class of 1992**.

"92 jie de" is the nominal predicate showing the characteristic of the subject as an agent who graduated in 1992. (5-17) to (5-19) present bare "shi" copula sentences acting the same function as "shi … de" copula sentences. From this, we can conclude that the focus in copula sentences, regardless of whether the copula verb "shi" is present, does not exhibit exhaustivity.

" Shi " emphatic sentences are distinguished from cleft sentences by, firstly, the exhaustivity of the focus, and secondly, the distribution of "presupposition" and "focus" from the perspective of information structure. To cite one example collected in the present study.

(5-20) 我想,当当是必须要上市的。
Wǒ xiǎng, dāngdāng shì bìxū yào shàngshì de.
1SG think Dangdang SHI$_{aux}$ must go public DE$_{ptcl}$.
I think that **Dangdang must go public**.

This sentence, although with both "shi" and "de", is only an emphatic sentence because, firstly, there is no exhaustive limitation for the focus constituent. The function of this sentence is to emphasize the confirmative mood of it by adding the auxiliary "shi" in the preceding position of the modal verb "必须 (have to)". The focus of the sentence is the proposition "当当必须要上市 (Dangdang must go public)", and there is no presupposition in the sentence. The function of this emphatic sentence is to highlight the confirmative modality of the sentence. Secondly, the distribution of the focus and the presupposition is another criterion reflecting one of the distinguished features of cleft sentences both in English and Chinese, and it is closely related to the exhaustivity of focus, for only if the focus is a constituent (instead of the proposition), could it be exhaustive.

This type of emphatic sentence is observed in the corpus, alongside another distinct type of emphatic construction. We designate (5-20) as "shi emphatic sentence — Type 1", which functions to highlight the sentence modality by preceding the modal element within the sentence. In contrast, the second type, referred to as "shi emphatic sentence — Type 2", serves to emphasize the truth value of the entire proposition.

For instance, consider an example of Type 2.

(5-21) A: 太阳是从东边升起吗?
A: Tàiyáng shì cóng dōngbiān shēngqǐ ma?
Sun SHI$_{aux}$ from east rise Q?

Does the sun rise from the east?

B: 太阳是从东边出来。

B: Tàiyáng shì cóng dōngbiān chūlái.

Sun SHI$_{aux}$ from east out.

The sun, indeed, comes out from the east.

Like the previous example, this sentence is an emphatic sentence with the whole sentence as the focus; however, the differences are: firstly, "shi" partners with prosodic prominence (without which, the sentence is only an explanatory copula sentence without any emphatic function) easily perceived by native speakers; secondly, instead of emphasizing the confirmative mood of the sentence, the function of this type of emphatic sentence is to affirm the truth-value of the sentence — "it is totally true that *the sun rises from the east*".

Although Type 1 and Type 2 emphatic sentences serve slightly different functions, they exhibit similar distributions of presupposition and focus. Specifically, both types share a null presupposition and take the entire sentence as the focus, neither of which is exhaustive. These two characteristics serve as key distinctions between "shi" emphatic sentences and Chinese cleft constructions.

Although many scholars (e.g., Lee, 2005; Shi, 1994) categorized "shi...de" sentences as emphatic constructions, this section aims to distinguish them from the perspective of exhaustivity. The variation in exhaustivity fundamentally stems from differences in the distribution of presupposition and focus.

The present corpus contains examples of both types of "shi" emphatic sentences, each serving distinct emphatic functions. Specifically, they either emphasize the truth value of the sentence or highlight the modality by drawing attention to modal elements, such as modal adverbs.

After the selection procedure, all the qualifying data are collected and based on the collected data, the following discussions are made to explain more about the information structure of Chinese cleft sentences.

Chapter 6 conducts the detailed analysis of the grammatical and informative interpretation of the focus of the Chinese cleft sentence, investigating the distributive relationship between the focused constituents and the information (given or new) from a sentence-structural perspective. Chapter 7 discusses the identifiability of focus and topic constituents of Chinese cleft sentences to probe how the information processors (i.e., hearer and listener) process the information, especially the prominent information aiming to deliver by cleft sentences.

Chapter 6

Grammatical and Informational Interpretations of Cleft Foci

In this section, two important components (i.e., the focus and topic) of the information structure of the Chinese cleft sentence are discussed. Detailed subjects discussed in this chapter are the following three aspects.

(i) The types of Chinese cleft sentences from the perspective of focus structure;

(ii) The configuration of the information structure of the collected data (i.e., the distribution of "presupposition" and "focus" in different types of Chinese cleft sentences);

(iii) The grammatical categories and definiteness of NPs involved in focus constituents.

In this chapter, Section 6.1 provides a comprehensive analysis of Chinese cleft sentence types by examining the focus domains of each construction. The discussion is supported by both empirical data and introspective examples to illustrate each category. Section 6.2 shifts the focus to the syntactic classifications of the focus constituents, offering a detailed examination of their structural properties. Building upon this foundation, Section 6.3 delves deeper into the grammatical categorization of nominal phrases within the identified focus domains, further refining the syntactic and semantic understanding of Chinese cleft constructions.

Chapter 6 Grammatical and Informational Interpretations of Cleft Foci

6.1 Focus Domains and Types of Focus Structures

As mentioned previously, Cleft sentences are marked constructions that are seldom used in discourse. Generally speaking, 110 cleft sentences in total are found, and against the hypothesis, the argument-cleft sentence would be the major group of cleft sentences in Chinese — only approximately 7% (n=8) of the cases are argument-focus clefts, while non-argument-focus cleft sentence exist overwhelmingly in the present corpus.

In the previous literature, there is no relevant investigation on the types of focus structure of Chinese cleft sentences. Moreover, discussions in English do not address the distinctions between argument-focus cleft sentences and other types.

Among previous studies on Chinese cleft constructions, numerous examples can be identified as argument-focus cleft sentences. However, corpus-based analysis reveals that in actual usage, non-argument-focus cleft sentences occur with significantly higher frequency than their argument-focus counterparts.

6.1.1 Argument–focus cleft sentences

In this study, only eight instances of sentences with argument foci were identified. This section presents both empirical and introspective examples, offering an informative analysis of their characteristics.

(6-1) 元元仰着头问:"把我要弹的曲子;录下来,好吗? <u>是朴哥哥教我的</u>。"

Yuan yuan tilted his head and asked, "Record the piece I'm going to play; record it, okay? It's <u>**Brother Park** who taught me the song</u>."

"Brother Park" is the argument of the action "teach" and also the focus constituent of the cleft sentence. It completes the assertion "It's Brother Park who taught me the song" by combining the focus and the presupposition "someone (X) taught me the song". It is a typical pattern of "shi ... de" argument-focus cleft sentence.

In Chinese cleft sentences, the object cannot serve as the focus, which constitutes a key characteristic of this construction. This structural constraint leads to the conclusion that, irrespective of contextual factors, argument-focus cleft sentences in Chinese predominantly manifest as subject-focus cleft sentences. The following example (6-4) presents the unacceptability of the object-focused situation.

(6-2) 小明**打破窗户了**。
Xiǎomíng dǎpò chuānghù le.
Xiaoming break window LE$_{aspc}$.
Xiaoming **broke the window**.

(6-3) 是小明打破窗户的。
Shì Xiǎomíng dǎpò chuānghù de.
SHI$_{aux}$ Xiaoming break window DE$_{ptcl}$.
It is **Xiaoming** who broke the window.

(6-4) *小明打破是窗户的。
*Xiǎomíng dǎpò shì chuānghù de.
*Xiaoming broke SHI$_{aux}$window DE$_{ptcl}$.

(6-5) 小明打破的是**窗户**。
Xiǎomíng dǎpò de shì chuānghù.
Xiaoming break DE$_{rel}$ SHI$_{cop}$ window.
What Xiaoming broke is **the window**.

Sentence (6-2) is an unmarked Chinese sentence with indicative mood, aspect marker "le" and it satisfies the temporal sequence and the topic-prominence of Modern Standard Chinese. Sentence (6-3) is the argument-focus cleft version of the canonical sentence (6-2). The focus domain of (6-3) acts as the argument of the sentence which, at the same time, it is the subject of the sentence in the form of a proper noun "Xiaoming". Sentence (6-4) is ungrammatical, indicating that, in terms of information structure, the object of a sentence cannot be focalized using the "shi … de" cleft construction. In other words, as a focus marker, "shi" can only appear in a preverbal position. However, pseudo-cleft sentence[①] (6-5) is both grammatically correct and informa- tionally acceptable.

To provide a broader perspective on argument-focus cleft sentences, two examples from other sources are cited here.

(6-6) 我有如此一个美的梦想,这梦想是<u>凌吉士</u>给我的。[②]

Wǒ yǒu rúcǐ yí gè měi de mèngxiǎng, zhè mèngxiǎng shì Líng Jíshì gěi wǒ de

1SG have such a beautiful DE$_{modi}$ dream, this dream SHI$_{aux}$ Ling jishi give 1SG DE$_{ptcl}$.

I have such a beautiful dream. It is **Ling Jishi** who gave me this dream.

This sentence is a topicalized argument-focus cleft sentence, with the canonical sentence being:

(6-7) 凌吉士给我这梦想。

Líng Jíshì gěi wǒ zhè mèngxiǎng.

Lingjishi give 1SG this dream.

Lingjishi gave me this dream.

The object "dream" is preposed to the initial position of the sentence, and this phenomenon is called topicalization. Topicalization is defined main-

---

[①] Pseudo-cleft sentences in Chinese put the object of the sentence as the focus of the sentence. Unlike cleft sentences, whose focus constituents may vary from one type to another according to different focus domains (except for the object), pseudo-cleft sentences only have one type—object cleft sentences. Besides, the classifications of "shi" and "de" are different in the pseudo-cleft sentence of Chinese compared with those in cleft sentences. Chinese pseudo-cleft sentences act as a type of copula sentence aiming to assign one and the only entity/identity represented by the constituent following "shi" to the subject, which is often modified by the relative pronoun "de".

[②] This example is quoted from 《莎菲女士的日记》 (Miss Sophies Diary) by Ding Ling.

ly syntactically as the movement of an element other than the subject to the left edge of the sentence (cf. Prince 1986, p. 218). However, the syntactic movement may generate two different functions. It may encode the topichood of the fronted element, or express contrastive focality. Whichever way this is done, the "prominent" meaning is expressed. To cite one example of topicalization from Ross (1967, p. 168).

(6-8) Beans **I don't like**.

The unmarked order is: "I don't like beans". By preposing the object of the sentence, the sentence aims to put the object in a more prominent position and thus realize the function of the sentence — to show the topichood of the object "beans" and make the listener aware that it is the specific part the speaker wants to highlight in particular by putting it at a prominent position. However, focus may also be topicalized as in the following example.

(6-9) **Fido** they named their dog. (Prince, 1981, p. 259)

Semantically, the exhaustive focus is always generated by the following mechanism: firstly, there is a set of alternatives of focus constituents; secondly, a variable or an element in the set is chosen as the exact variable suitable for the value expressed by the sentence. In this example, the alternative set is the set of dog names such as {Fido, Jessica, Jack, Cooper, Lola, Harley, etc.}; and "Fido" is the one and the only variable is chosen as the focus of the sentence.

To distinguish these two types of "topicalization", Prince (1981) named the first one "topicalization" (i.e., example 6-8) and the latter "focus movement" (i.e., 6-9). However, Badan and Del Gobbo (2011) argued that Chinese lacks a "topicalized" focus movement, as exemplified in sentences (6-9). Their empirical analysis demonstrated that the movement of contrastive or exhaustive focus to the left periphery in Chinese is not generally accepted by native speakers.

Building on their perspective, the topicalization observed in sentences (6-8) is best understood as a manifestation of topic movement. This suggests that the initial nominal phrase, "this dream," functions as the topic rather than the focus of the sentence. Furthermore, the topicalized movement does not affect the focal structure of the sentence, as the focus remains with the constituent immediately following the focus marker "shi". The information struc- ture of the sentence is shown in Table 6-1.

(6-10) 这梦想是**凌吉士**给我的。
Zhè mèngxiǎng shì Líng Jíshì gěi wǒ de.
This dream SHI$_{aux}$ Lingjishi give 1SG DE$_{ptcl}$.
It is **Ling Jishi** who gave me this dream.

Table 6-1 Configuration of the information structure of the example sentence (6-10)

这梦想 This dream	是 SHI$_{aux}$	凌吉士 Ling Jishi	给我 gave me	的。 DE$_{ptcl}$
Presupposition$_i$ (The existance of the dream)	–	Focus(X)	Presupposition$_i$ [someone (X) gave me this dream]	–
Assertion				

In a topic-prominent language like Chinese or Japanese, object topicalization should be related to the passive[①] because it can perform the following two functions.

(i) to foregrounds the patient.

(ii) to de-topicalizes the agent.

In this passive sentence, the ending particle "de" is a past tense[②] marker

---

[①] It is generally accepted that Chinese does not have the passive voice from the perspective of syntax defined by traditional scholars. "Only if we look at passives from the point of view of pragmatics and define passives as constructions which defocus the agent and emphasize the affectedness of the patient (Shibatani, 1985) can Chinese be said to have passives" (Lapolla, 1988). Noonan and Woock (1978) named this type of passive the functional passive. The functional passive is realized by changing the word order, certain referential properties, and the orientation of a sentence, but does not change grammatical functions.

[②] It is widely accepted that Chinese is a language without tense morphology. However Chinese does have tense-aspect particles, and some pragmatic reasoning to determine the temporal interpretation of sentences (Li, 1999; Lin, 2003, 2005; Smith and Erbaugh, 2005).

representing the completed status of the action shown by the main verb. If "de" acts as the tense marker of the sentence, the omission of "de" causes the ungrammatical reading of the original sentence.

(6-11) *这梦想是凌吉士给我。

*Zhè mèngxiǎng shì Líng Jíshì gěi wǒ.

*This dream SHIaux give me.

(6-12) 老孙赶着老杜家的大车,常对人们说:"<u>工作队长是**我接来的**</u>。"[1]

Driving Lao Du's cart, Lao Sun often said to the people: "It was **I** who brought the working team leader here".

The same topicalized phenomenon happens to this sentence as well. Very similarly, the information structure of the sentence goes like this (see Table 6-2).

Table 6-2 Configuration of the information structure of the example sentence (6-12)

工作队长 The working team leader	是 SHI$_{aux}$	我 me	接来 brought here	的。 DE$_{ptcl}$.
Topic	–	Focus	–	–
presupposition$_i$	–	X	presupposition$_i$	–
Assertion				

The canonical sentence is:

(6-13) 我接来工作队长。

Wǒ jiēlái gōngzuò duìzhǎng.

I 1SG bring here working team leader.

I brought the working team leader here.

In this case as well, the focalized constituent is the subject of the canonical sentence.

Besides, "ba" and "bei" structures are also typical forms of argument-

---

[1] This example is quoted from 《暴风骤雨》 (The Hurrican) by Zhou Libo.

focus cleft sentences. The following examples are collected from the present study. Here, the differences between "bei sentence" and "ba sentence" are discussed from the perspective of information structure.

(6-14) "哦,你们在那里呀！我在监狱里找不到你,我还以为你已经逃了。" "是**我的一些部属**救我出来的。"
"Oh, there you are! I couldn't find you in prison, and I thought you had escaped." "It was **some of my subordinate** who saved" me.

(6-15) 我的一些部属**把我救出来了**。
Wǒ de yìxiē bùshǔ bǎ wǒ jiù chūlái le.
1SG DE$_{poss}$ some subordinate BA$_{prep}$ 1SG rescue-out LE$_{aspc}$.
Some of my subordinates **rescued me**.

(6-16) 我的一些部属**救我出来了**。
Wǒ de yìxiē bùshǔ jiù wǒ chūlái le.
1SG DE$_{poss}$ some subordinate rescue 1SG out LEaspc.
Some of my subordinates **rescued me**.

Before getting into specific comparisons, let me briefly explain sentences expressing "causative meaning". According to the "*Construction-chunk*" approach, sentences that express the concept of "causation" consist of four semantic construction chunks — the causer (Agent), the object of the causative action (Patient), the method of the causative action, and the result of causative action.

In causative "ba" sentences, the following observations are made: firstly, the topic should be the causer [i.e., "some of my ministers" in sentence (6-15)]; secondly, the focus of the discussion should be on the "result of the causative action" (i.e., "saved me"); thirdly, the use of the preposition "把（BA）" can help freely introduce the "object of the causative action" (i.e., "me") into the sentence, while also indicating the strong influence of the "causative action" and the speaker's subjective perspective, thus highlighting the "result".

Sentence (6-16) is the canonical "subject+verb+object" sentence with the verbal constituent "救我出来" being the informative focus of the sentence. It is a statement clarifying the state of fact. But this canonical sentence is inserted into the "shi … de" sentence putting particular focus on the post-shi position. As Liu and Xu (1998) stated, within one clause, it is impossible to have the contrastive focus and the informative focus at the same time, usually, the contrastive focus would supersede the informative focus and act as the main focus of the clause. The informative focus of (6-16) is converted into the argument and contrastive focus in cleft sentence (6-14).

The "bei" and "ba" sentences are both used to highlight the "patient" of the sentence, who is both the focus and topic in respective sentences. The ba-sentence emphasizes the "patient" by putting it to the beginning of the sentence, leaving the "agent" in the topic position. On the other hand, the bei-sentence promotes the "patient" to the topic position.

From the above examples, we can conclude that.

Firstly, the occurrence of argument-focus cleft sentences is relatively rare, with such constructions accounting for only 7% of the collected data.

Secondly, evidence from additional data collected from various sources[①] (e.g., novels and essays) suggests that topicalization is a prevalent feature in argument-focus cleft sentences. When considered alongside the first finding, this indicates that argument-focus cleft sentences in Chinese consistently exhibit a marked syntactic structure.

Thirdly, the presupposition of an argument-focus cleft sentence takes the form of a proposition. However, it specifically functions as an existential proposition, in which the subject is an unidentified person or entity, often represented by "x." Notably, in contrast to other focus structures — such as predicate-focus constructions, whose presuppositions are often incomplete propositions — the presupposition of an argument-focus cleft sentence is fully formed and structurally complete.

[①] The data collected from external sources, as well as introspective data, are not included in the core results of this study. Instead, they serve as supplementary materials for data analysis.

Lastly, "ba" and "bei" constructions are frequently employed to restructure the information structure of canonical Chinese sentences, facilitating their transformation into cleft constructions.

6.1.2 Adjunct–focus cleft sentences

The prerequisite of Lambrecht's (1994) categories of focus structures is the semantic division between the argument and predicate of the sentence. This division is recognized and adopted in the present study. However, this division alone is not sufficiently comprehensive to account for the full range of cleft sentence types in Chinese. As discussed in Chapter 5, the adjunct-focus structure also constitutes a significant category of Chinese cleft sentences and warrants further consideration.

By analyzing the grammatical roles of the focus constituents, we conclude that all the non-argument cleft sentences involved in this present study are adjunct cleft sentences. Their functions are to elaborate the *manner/purpose/place/time*, etc. of the action by treating them as the focus of the sentence. Unlike their English counterparts, Chinese cleft sentences do not involve syntactic movement. Instead, focus constituents in Chinese cleft constructions are primarily marked by the insertion of the focus marker "shi" preceding them.

The focused adjunct can be in various syntactic categories such as APs, VPs, PPs, etc. Here I take several examples from the collected data to show that the differences between adjunct-focus cleft sentences and argument-focus cleft sentences mainly fall on two aspects: firstly, the different focus domains; and secondly, different configurative relationships between presupposition and focus.

(6-17) 陈存仪是**在抓住刘招华后的第一时间**由北京飞抵福建的。
Chén Cúnyí shì zài zhuāzhù Liú Zhāohuá hòu de dì-yī shíjiān yóu Běijīng fēidǐ Fújiàn de.

Chen Cunyi SHI$_{aux}$ at catch Liu Zhaohua DE$_{modi}$ first time from Beijing fly to Fujian DE$_{ptcl}$.
Chen cunyi flew back to Fujian from Beijing **immediately after Liuzhaohua being caught**.

"Immediately after Liuzhaohua being caught" is the focus constituent of this cleft sentence. The head noun of this constituent or clause is actually "immdediately", and "after Liuzhaohua being caught" is the preceding modifying constituent linked to the head noun by the modifier "de". The focus is self-contained information in which some constituent is evoked dependently on the other one (see Table 6-3).

The presupposition of the sentence — "Chen Cunyi arrived Beijing from Fujian" is a completed proposition already.

The focus of this type of cleft sentence acts as the adjunct of the sentence, the omission of the focus from the sentence does not make the sentence an ungrammatical one.

Table 6-3 Configuration of the information structure of the example sentence (6-17)

陈存仪 Chen Cunyi	是 SHI$_{aux}$	在抓住刘招华后的第一时间 immediately after Liu Zhaohua being caught	由北京飞抵福建 flew back to Fujian from Beijing	的。 DE$_{ptcl}$.
Topic	–	Focus	–	–
presupposition$_i$	–	X	presupposition$_i$	–
Assertion				

(6-18) 男人的面子有时候是**自己挣出来**的,有时候是**别人给出来**的。

A man's face is sometimes **earned by his own achievements**, and it is sometimes **given by others**.

The contrastive focus constituent of the two cleft sentences is the VPs "earned by his own achievements" and "given by others". The latter paralleling clause provides the focus reading for both of the clauses.

For derailed information, please see Table 6-4.

Table 6-4 Configuration of the information structure of the example sentence (6-18)

男人的面子有时候 A man's face is sometimes	是 SHI$_{aux}$	自己挣出来 earned by his own achievements		的。 DE$_{ptcl.}$
Topic	–	Focus		–
presupposition$_i$	–	X	presupposition$_i$	–
Assertion				

Table 6-4' Configuration of the information structure of the example sentence (6-18)

有时候 A man's face is sometimes	是 SHI$_{aux}$	别人给出来 given by others		的。 DE$_{ptcl.}$
Topic	–	Focus		–
presupposition$_i$	–	X	presupposition$_i$	–
Assertion				

6.2 Syntactic Categories of Focus Constituents

The syntactic categories of focus constituents in Chinese cleft sentences include verbal phrases, nominal phrases, adverbial phrases, prepositional phrases, etc. The distributions of the categories are presented in the following Figure 6-1.

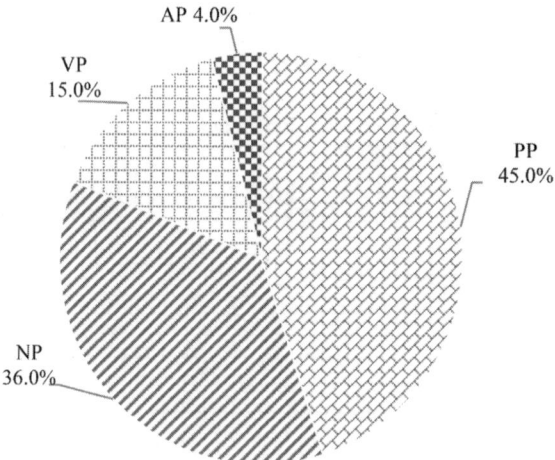

Figure 6-1 Syntactic categories of focus constituents of Chinese cleft sentences

Among the cleft constituents in Chinese cleft sentences analyzed in this study, 45% are prepositional phrases, making them the most frequently occurring focus constituents. Nominal phrases rank second, while verbal phrases account for 15% of the cases. Adverbial phrases are the least common among the four categories.

6.3 Grammatical Categories of Nominal Phrases in Focus Domains

This section aims to make an investigation of all the NPs[①] involved in focus constituents by checking their grammatical categories of the nominal forms and their identifiability/ referentiality.

Regarding the semantic referentiality and definiteness of Chinese NPs, Chen (2017) gave a persuasive and comprehensive discussion summarized by the Table 6-5.

---

① From the grammar perspective, the premise of definiteness and identifiability should be nominal or any constituent that projects a nominal (i.e., PP=preposition + noun, etc.). That means if the focus of a sentence is neither an NP nor any construction projecting a noun, the sentence is excluded from the analysis of the following chapters.

Table 6-5 Semantic referentiality of grammatical categories of Chinese NPs (Chen, 2017, p.241)

	Semantic referential	Semantic nonreferential
Definite		
proper NP	+	-
personal pronoun	+	-
demonstrative *zhe/na* 'this/that'	+	-
zhe/na 'this/that'+NP	+	+
Indefinite		
yi 'one'+(CL)+NP	+	+
CL+NP		
Indeterminate		
numeral/*ji* 'several'...+CL+NP	+	+
bare NP	+	+
Partitive quantifier		
mei 'each', 'every'	-	+
suoyou 'all'	-	+
yiqie 'all'	-	+
daduoshu 'majority', 'most'	-	+
duoshu 'most'	-	+
shaoshu 'few'		

In Chinese, the pragmatic difference between identifiability and non-identifiability is conveyed through specific lexical and morphological encoding, as well as through the positioning of noun phrases within sentences.

Chen (2017) summarized the identifiability/ referentiality of Chinese NPs into definite, indefinite, and indeterminate groups.

Demonstratives, one of the major definite determiners in Chinese, serve to identify referents through shared general knowledge and in anaphoric and associative uses. However, they still retain their deictic force to a significant extent in these situations.

The main marker of indefiniteness in Chinese is the classifier "yi" which serves functions similar to those of indefinite articles in English and has even more functions beyond that. Different from the articles in English, the definite and indefinite determiners in Chinese have not fully acquired the status of specialized grammatical markers of definiteness and indefiniteness in terms of morphology and function.

Possessives in Chinese display features similar to adjectival-genitive (AG) languages such as Italian rather than determiner-genitive (DG) languages like English, but they also have unique features not shared by typical AG languages.

The Chinese language is distinguished from English by the presence of what the writer calls "indeterminate expressions". These expressions consist of *bare noun* phrases and *cardinality* expressions, and their interpretation in terms of identifiability is influenced by their position in sentences. It is noted that the lexical and morphological encoding of these expressions is neutral concerning identifiability, and it is the sentence structure that indicates whether they are meant to be interpreted as identifiable or nonidentifiable.

Certain positions in Chinese sentences are more likely to be associated with definite expressions, while others are more likely to be associated with indefinite expressions. For indeterminate expressions, there is a strong but not absolute correlation between their interpretation in terms of identifiability and their position in the sentence. When nominal expressions are encoded in determinate lexical and morphological terms, their status as identifiable is clear, but when indeterminate expressions are used, the speaker expects the addressee to infer their interpretation in terms of identifiability based on various factors, including the expression's topicality, the availability of a referent that matches its descriptive content, and other relevant information in the discourse.

This section explores the identifiable relationship between informational roles (i.e., focus) and grammatical categories, seeking to determine whether the focusing effect gives rise to any underlying rules that govern the identifiable readings of nominals within the focus domain.

6.3.1 Nominal forms

To analyze the definiteness and identifiability of nominal phrases, the first step is to define key concepts and provide a systematic explanation of different nominal forms.

6.3.1.1 Bare nouns

In Chinese, a non-inflectional language, bare nouns frequently appear in both discourse and spoken utterances. Bare nouns refer to nouns used without any articles or other words that indicate their grammatical function. Bare nouns attract many discussions about their different semantic interpretations (i.e., generic reading, definite and indefinite readings) regarding locations and context. The widely accepted tendency of the referential readings of bare nouns are as follows in Chinese: in the preverbal position, bare nouns can be interpreted as definite or generic, but not as indefinite; in the postverbal position, Mandarin bare nouns can be interpreted as indefinite, definite or generic. To quote some examples from Cheng and Sybesma (1999, p.510).

(6-19) a. Hufei mǎi *shū* qù le.
Hufei buy book go LE$_{aspc}$.
"Hufei went to buy *a book/ books*." — indefinite
b. Hufei he-wan-le *tang*.
Hufei drink-finish-LE$_{aspc}$ soup.
"Hufei finished *the soup*". — definite
c. Wo xihuan *gou*.
I like *dog*. –generic

(6-20) a. * 狗要过马路。
Gǒu yào guò mǎlù.
Dog want to cross road.
*A dog wants to cross the road.
b. 狗今天特别听话。

Gǒu jīntiān tèbié tīnghuà.

Dog today especially be obedient.

The dog/ dogs was/were especially obedient today.

c. 狗爱吃肉。

Gǒu ài-chī ròu.

Dog love eat meat.

Dogs love to eat meat.

In Chinese, bare nouns can have different referential interpretations — indefinite, definite, or generic — which influences their acceptability in certain constructions. Sentence (6-20)a 狗要过马路 ("A dog wants to cross the road") is ungrammatical because the bare noun "狗" cannot express an indefinite subject (a dog) without a determiner like "一只 (English 'a')". Sentence (6-20)b 狗今天特别听话 ("The dog was especially obedient today") is grammatical and features an indefinite but identifiable interpretation of "狗 (dog)". Sentence (6-20)c 狗爱吃肉 ("Dogs love to eat meat") represents a generic statement, where the bare noun refers to the kind as a whole. These examples highlight how the referential status of a bare noun impacts information structure and the types of constructions it may appear in.

This section examines the referential interpretation of bare nouns in light of the following two key factors. First, in this study, "shi" is regarded both as an auxiliary and a focus marker that highlights the focus constituent following it. In most cases, the focus constituent appears between "shi" and the verb, meaning that the majority of bare nouns functioning as focus constituents receive pre-verbal referential readings. Second, all bare nouns analyzed in this section fall within the focus domain. Given the close relationship between referentiality and information structure (i.e., topic and focus), this raises the question: Does the referential reading of a focused bare noun depend on its information structure?

6.3.1.2 Proper nouns

Similar to proper nouns in English[①], those of Chinese elicit definite readings. Chinese proper nouns are names given to specific people, places, or things in the Chinese language.

Proper nouns refer to the shared concepts/ entity/ person etc. by communicators holding the same cultural and social background, so in most cases, they are expressions showing identifiable and definite referents.

6.3.1.3 Demonstrative +nouns

Demonstratives differ from definite articles in two major ways. Firstly, definite articles function only adjectivally, whereas demonstratives may function adjectivally, pronominally, and adverbially. Secondly, the primary function of demonstratives in English is deixis, which has also been expanded to other uses. This means that demonstratives are used to locate and identify entities concerning their spatial and temporal position in relation to the speech participants. As determiners of definiteness, they are typically used deictically, indicating to the listener in some way that the referent being discussed is accessible to them based on the position of the participants in the discourse. Definite articles, on the other hand, are not deictic in nature.

According to Himmelmann (1996), demonstratives have four different types of usages, here list some examples borrowed from Chen (2004).

I. Situational

(6-21)　Could you please give me a hand with *this* big box?

II. Discourse deictic

(6-22)　He did not answer our phone call as promised. *This* is not good.

III. Anaphoric

(6-23)　There is a zoo a couple of miles down the road. You won't see many animals in *that* zoo.

[①] Definite expressions in English include three categories—definite NPs, proper nouns, and personal pronouns.

IV. Recognitional

(6-24)　It was filmed in California, *those* dusky kind of hills that they have out here by Stockton and all.

Demonstratives used in recognitional contexts are utilized to refer to things or ideas that have been previously mentioned in a conversation or to introduce new ones. This usage combines the characteristics of definite determiners that rely on shared knowledge and those that stand on their own. The speaker assumes that the addressee shares some knowledge about the referent but still tries to provide enough identifying information to help the addressee identify it.

In Chinese, the definite article "the" does not exist. Instead, according to Chen (2004), three main types of definite determiners are used to indicate that a referent is identifiable, aside from proper nouns and personal pronouns. These determiners include demonstratives, possessives, and universal quantifiers.

However, although definite articles typically evolve from demonstratives, the grammaticalization of the Chinese demonstratives "这" (this) / "那" (that) is not as advanced as that of the definite article "the" in English. Nevertheless, "那 (that)" exhibits a higher degree of grammaticalization compared to "这 (this)" in Chinese.

6.3.1.4　Possessive nouns

As mentioned previously, possessive nouns are often treated as definite determiners. When a bare NP (unmarked for identifiability) is the head of a nominal expression in Chinese, the possessive form of the language can indicate the definiteness of the noun phrase.

However, determining whether a nominal phrase in Chinese containing a possessive and a bare noun refers to something specific or not depends on whether there is an indefinite determiner between the possessive and the bare noun. In Chinese grammar, it is perfectly acceptable to include an indefinite determiner in that position. When it is not present, it strongly suggests that the nominal phrase refers to something specific, which can be explained in terms of Gricean *conversational implicature* (cf. Grice, 1989; Levinson, 2000).

6.3.1.5　Yi+classifier+ nouns

As Chen (2004) stated, the most important indefinite determiner in Chinese is the "yi+classifier".

In contrast to the other numerals, the "yi+classifier" has undergone a process of grammaticalization that has turned it into a marker of indefiniteness, similar to how the English indefinite article evolved from the numeral "one." Although the "yi+classifier" can function as both a pronoun and a determiner, it fulfils all the major roles of a typical indefinite article, such as "a" in English, and also includes other uses that are not observed in indefinite determiners of any language.

Chinese differs from other languages in terms of definiteness markers, as it does not have a simple, fully grammaticalized marker for definiteness like the definite article in English. While Chinese demonstratives share certain functions with definite articles in other languages, their primary role is not as deictically neutral markers of definiteness, as seen with "the" in English. Although the Chinese numeral "yi" has possibly reached the endpoint of grammaticalization into an indefinite article, there is no contrast between it and a highly grammaticalized marker of definiteness. Additionally, unlike in English, marking a nominal expression as either definite or indefinite is not mandatory in Chinese. Due to the abundance of situations in which the interpretation of bare noun phrases and cardinality expressions cannot be determined solely based on their position in sentences, and may even be ambiguous or indeterminate with regard to identifiability, definiteness, and indefiniteness cannot be clearly specified for nominal expressions in Chinese. Therefore, it can be concluded that definiteness has not been fully developed as a grammatical category in Chinese in the narrow sense of the term. In the present study, the definiteness and identifiability are discussed within the domain of Chinese cleft sentences functioning to focus some constituents under speakers' intention.

6.3.2 Results and explanations

Although the dataset is limited in size, the Figure 6-2 clearly illustrates that proper nouns are the most frequent nominal type among cleft focus constituents. Modifier nouns rank second, followed by bare nouns, while demonstrative + NP constructions occur least frequently. The following section provides examples of each type for further elaboration.

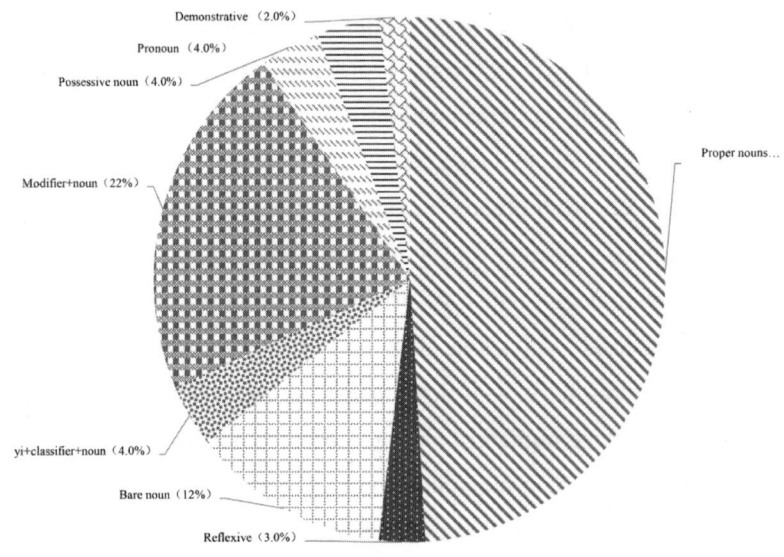

Figure 6-2 Grammatical categories of the nominal phrases in the focus domain of Chinese cleft sentences

6.3.2.1 Proper nouns

As mentioned previously, proper nouns in both English and Chinese are considered definite referring expressions whose indicated referents are identifiable for both the speaker and the hearer.

(6-25) 我那个大孙子去年考上了大学,建筑工程学院,<u>他是六十五中毕业的</u>,这孩子们都挺,都挺有出息的。

My eldest grandson got accepted into university last year.

He's attending the School of Architecture and Engineering. He graduated from *No. 65 Middle School*. These kids are all remarkable and have bright futures ahead of them.

"No. 65 Middle School" here is a proper noun that is and should be shared by both the speaker and hearer, this shared situation is at least assumed by the speaker before the utterance is made, and considering the successful encoding of the utterance (the listener does not put this referent "No. 65 Middle School" under discussion[①] in the subsequent discourse).

Most of the other cases holding proper nouns in their focus domain are time nouns showing the function of reporting the time of the action in the sentence, as in the following example:

(6-26) 不过,我们这一代知识分子,毕竟与我们的老师辈不太相同。我们是**解放以后**成长起来的。

However, our generation of intellectuals is quite different from the older generation of our teachers. We grew up after *the liberation*.

"Liberation" is a proper noun shared by all Chinese native speakers, it is identifiable due to the shared-knowledge and is definite from a syntactic perspective.

For the data of the present study, proper nouns are identifiable based on the shared knowledge of communicators possessing the same cultural and social background.

---

① The concept of "Question Under Discussion" is proposed and discussed by Roberts (1996), Ginzburg (1996), and Groenendijk (1999). The main idea behind this concept is that discourse can be thought of as a series of questions and answers, which address sub-issues of the current topic of conversation until all such issues are resolved. At any given point in the discourse, there is a current Question Under Discussion (QUD) that the interlocutors are attempting to resolve, either directly or by addressing a series of sub-questions. These sub-questions together provide a full resolution of the current QUD.

6.3.2.2 Modifier +nouns

It is widely accepted that comparing with bare nouns, it is easier for listeners to identify the referent indicated by the modifier+bare noun, and the more modifiers there are, the less effort the listeners would pay.

(6-27) 对于高管离职,离职的成本更高。能够做到高级管理职位说明你受公司的重视。如果你<u>是**在非正常状态下走的**</u>,对现在公司可能造成较大伤害。

For executives, the cost of leaving the company is higher. Attaining a senior management position indicates that you are valued by the company. <u>If you leave **under *abnormal circumstances***</u>, it may cause significant harm to the current company.

"Abnormal circumstances" includes a modifier "abnormal" and a bare noun "circumstances". In this sentence, it is put in the focus position to show the speakers' intention to give particular prominence.

6.3.2.3 Bare nouns

(6-28) 他不是很壮,体力上天赋不好。他投篮好,球感好,<u>他是用脑子打球的</u>。

He is not very strong and does not have good physical aptitude; however, he is good at shooting and has a good feel for basketball. <u>He plays basketball **using *his brain***</u>.

"Brain" in Chinese is a bare noun instead of the possessive phrase "his brain" as in the English translation. In this case, the bare noun falls in the focus domain, showing the newness of the information expressed by the structure. As known by the literature, Chinese bare nouns show indeterminate definiteness depending on the information structure. In this sentence, "brain" here is identifiable by the hearer in accordance with the inference –"the speaker is talking about the wisdom of Yaoming".

6.3.2.4 Yi+classifier+nouns

(6-29) 小说的第一句话我是**坐在一辆自行车上写下的**。
The first sentence of the novel was written **while I was sitting on** *a bicycle*.

"Yi+classifier+NP" is an indefinite expression in Chinese, and the phrase is in the focus domain describing new information in this example.

6.3.2.5 Possessive nouns

(6-30) "哦,你们在那里呀！我在监狱里找不到你,我还以为你已经逃了。""是**我的一些部属救我出来的**。"
"Oh, there you are! I couldn't find you in prison, and I thought you had escaped."" It was **some of my subordinates** who rescued me."

This example is mentioned before. Possessive nouns are considered definite expressions in Chinese, and this possessive phrase falls in the focus domain of the sentence expressing new information of the sentence.

6.3.2.6 Pronouns

(6-31) （如果我没记错的话,）昨天是**你**为他提行李上楼的。
If I remember correctly, it was **you** who helped him carry the luggage upstairs.

This is a very typical example of an argument-focus cleft sentence. Pronouns are highly identifiable for their definite feature, and in this sentence, the pronoun is the focus constituent. The pronoun "you" in this sentence is a deixis that is identifiable for the listener of the current utterance.

6.3.2.7 Reflexives

Reflexives are typical anaphor in both Chinese and English, they are active for their definiteness. Chomsky's *Government and Binding* theory claims that reflexive as the anaphor, must be bound by an antecedent within the same sentence.

(6-32) 不管有没有好的条件,好的身材是靠自己创造的。
No matter whether there are good conditions or not, a good physique is created **by** *oneself*.

Reflexive, as the anaphor, in this sentence, is not bounded within the sentence, but for listeners, "oneself" here is identifiable and known as all the listeners themselves.

6.3.2.8 Demonstrative+nouns

(6-33) 我不是只告计程车司机的,我是从那个国民党伪总统一路告起。
I didn't only sue the taxi driver, I sued **from** *that bogus president of the Kuomintang party*.

Demonstrative nouns in Chinese are definite, in this case, "demonstrative+proper noun" is identifiable for listeners sharing mutual knowledge background.

6.4 Discussion and Summary

This chapter pays attention to the relationship between grammatical forms and the information delivery of focus constituents. According to the data collected, most Chinese cleft sentences are adjunct-focus sentences with the focus being the description, modification, or explanation of any aspects of the action expressed in the sentence.

Regarding the grammatical classes of focus constituents of Chinese cleft sentences in this study, prepositional phrases rank first, then follow by nominal phrases, verbal phrases, and adverbial phrases. On the syntactic categories of NPs in focus domains, proper nouns account for the highest proportion, and modifier+nouns rank second, while bare nouns rank third.

The relationship between the definiteness of the grammatical categories of foci in Chinese cleft sentences and their informative role — the focus of the sentence, proposes the necessity of discussing the relationship between the grammatical form (i.e., definiteness) and information structure from a pragmatic perspective.

6.4.1 Necessity of pragmatic explanations of Chinese cleft sentences

Shen (2017) advocated that Chinese grammar should be analyzed in a different way from grammars of Indo-European languages.

The relationship between grammar and usage in Chinese is more complex than some western scholars have suggested. It is not just a matter of grammar being grammar and usage being usage or vice versa, but rather that grammar is a part of usage and cannot be separated from it. Without considering usage, the discussion of grammar in Chinese would be limited, as the categories and units of grammar are formed by the categories and units of usage. It is proposed that the analysis of Chinese grammar should be approached from three interrelated perspectives — grammar, semantics, and pragmatics. Rather than being treated as isolated components, these three aspects should be integrated into a unified and cooperative model. The relationship between grammar and pragmatic usages of Chinese and Indo-European languages is shown by the Figure 6-3.

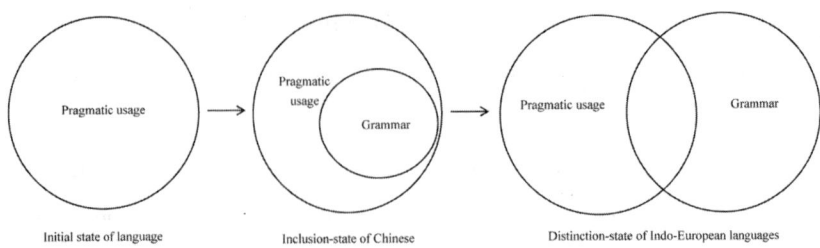

Figure 6-3 The relationship between grammar and pragmatic usages of Chinese and Indo-European languages (Shen, 2017, p.5)

To analyze the grammar of Chinese cleft sentences from a pragmatic perspective, a productive starting point is to examine how information is structured and conveyed within these sentences.

6.4.2 Relationship between definiteness and focus

Through the observation of the definiteness of NPs included in the focus domain of the cleft sentences in this study, we conclude that the definiteness of Chinese NPs does not have a direct and correlating relationship with focus, in other words, the focus of Chinese cleft sentences does not show the inclination of being definite or indefinite NPs.

Definiteness is a grammatical concept, whereas identifiability is a cognitive and pragmatic notion. Observations indicate that grammatically defined definite forms (e.g., pronouns), indefinite forms (e.g., yi + classifier + NP), and indeterminate forms (e.g., bare nouns) can all appear in similar syntactic positions (i.e., the focus domain) in Chinese cleft sentences. However, their degrees and types of identifiability vary, a topic that will be further explored in the following chapter.

6.4.3 Relationship between definiteness and new/given information

The word order of canonical declarative Chinese sentences follows the organization of information structure and is arranged from known to unknown. The subject in Chinese tends to be known or old information rather than a definite element.

The differentiation between topic and focus is often associated with the separation between given and new information within a sentence, however, confusion and disagreement still exist. Gundel (1988) introduced two terms "referential giveness-newness" and "relational givenness-newness"[①] to explain the disagreement.

Referential givenness-newness pertains to the relationship between a linguistic expression and a non-linguistic entity as perceived by the speaker or listener. This relationship manifests in discourse or utterance and may exist in either the real or an imagined world. Gundel and Fretheim (2004) considered the following concepts examples of referential givenness: existential presupposition (Strawson, 1964), various senses of referentiality and specificity (Fodor and Sag, 1982, Enç, 1991), the familiarity condition on definite descriptions (Heim, 1982), the activation and identifiability statuses proposed by Chafe (1994) and Lambrecht (1994).

In the context of language and sentence construction, the concept of "relational givenness-newness" refers to the division of a sentence into two parts: X and Y. X refers to what the sentence is about, while Y represents what is being asserted or questioned about X, or the predicate. X is considered given because it is independent of what is being said in Y, while Y is new because it contains information that is being asserted or questioned about X. This concept helps to determine the truth value of a sentence and is represented in various ways, including topic-comment and theme-rheme structures. The terms "topic" and "focus" are used in this context to refer to X and Y respectively. In Gundel's study, the structure of topic-focus is linked to relational givenness/ newness, which means that the topic is considered to

---

[①] Chu (2018) proposed another method to avoid confusion by adding a new concept—message to be the counterpart of "information". Guided by the method, the focus provides a "new message" (instead of the new information) to the topic.

be already known and the focus is the new information being conveyed about the topic.

Compared to referential givenness/newness, relational givenness/newness is more inherently a characteristic of linguistic representation. However, from the perspective of information structure, these two types of givenness/newness are interconnected and cannot be considered in isolation.

There are similarities and differences between known/ unknown information and definite/ indefinite reference. In Chinese declarative sentences, definite reference components and known information often appear in the front of the discourse, while indefinite reference and unknown information often appear in the back of the discourse. However, known/unknown information and definite/ indefinite reference do not completely overlap. Definite/ indefinite reference mainly applies to nominal elements, while known/unknown is a pattern of information structure that can be nominal or non-nominal. The focused constituent of the Chinese cleft sentence, who provides a new information (or in Chu's version, a new message) based on the topic and the sentence would have the forms of definite, indefinite, and indeterminate NPs in Chinese, this fact also supports the relationship between definiteness and information structure of Chinese summarized in Zhou's (2020) study (see Figure 6-4).

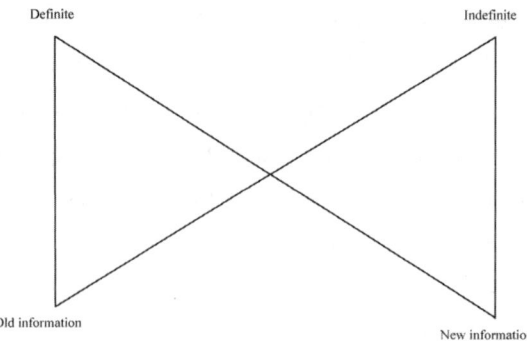

Figure 6-4 Relationship between definite/indefinite and new/given information (Zhou, 2020)

Although definiteness and givenness often overlap, definiteness does not necessarily indicate given information, nor does given information inherently imply definiteness. It is widely acknowledged that the primary distinction in information structure lies between new and given information, while the distinction between definite and indefinite is of secondary importance. And there is a consensus that, rather than asserting that Chinese subjects have a strong inclination towards definiteness, it is more accurate to say that they show a strong inclination towards given/known information.Similarly, this study finds that in Chinese cleft sentences, focus constituents tend to align more with new information rather than with indefiniteness.

Chapter 7

The Identifiability of the Focus and Topic Constituents in Chinese Cleft Sentences

This chapter examines two key aspects: the identifiability of focus and topic constituents, and the grammatical categories of noun phrases (NPs) in relation to their degree of identifiability[1]. The findings of this discussion establish a connection between information structure constituents (i.e., focus and topic) and the identifiable status of their referents.

7.1 The Distribution of Focus and Topic Constituents Across Identifiable Statuses

The identifiability/ definiteness of the grammatical form of a sentence constituent does not have a direct relationship with the identifiability of its reference. The latter is decided by the cognitive status of the hearer. Although the cognitive status of the hearer cannot be detected easily, the identifiability of the reference is perceivable for interlocuters. The identifiability is reflected by some grammatical and syntactic methods of a sentence or even a discourse.

As discussed in Chapter 4, the "identifiability" model proposed by Lambrecht (1994) is adjusted according to the data collected in the present

---

[1] In the previous chapter, the definiteness of various nominal categories was examined. This chapter shifts the attention to their identifiability.

study. The model of identifiability used in the present study is a combined one based on Lambrecht's (1994) and Chen's (2004) studies. Lambrecht's model categorizes the status of identifiability into "unidentifiable", "inactive", "accessible", "active", and "accessible" is further subcategorized into "textually", "situationally" and "inferentially" according to the way the constituent is accessed.

Chen (2004) proposed the cognitive basis of identifiability in his study.

"The status of being identifiable can be assumed by the speaker to have been established for an entity between him and the addressee under a variety of identificatory resources. Roughly speaking, they fall into two major categories. In the first category, identifiability is directly evoked from its presence in the context of discourse, composed of the physical situation of utterance and the linguistic text. In the second category, the identifiability of the entity in question is established based on shared background knowledge between the speaker and addressee or inferable from other entities in discourse by virtue of the knowledge shared by participants of the speech event about the associations between the former and the latter." (Chen, 2004, pp. 1136-1137)

He summarized that the uses of the English definite article fall into four major categories and some subcategories, and among all these categories, "shared general", "specific knowledge", "frame-based association", and "self-containing association" are the subtypes of the second cognitive basis mentioned in the last paragraph, which is quite similar to the "inferentially-accessible" category proposed by Lambrecht (1994).

In accordance with the data, it is found that Lambrecht's model cannot cover all cases in the present study; therefore, an integrated model is established by borrowing some of Chen's (2004) criteria. The new model is as follows (see Figure 7-1).

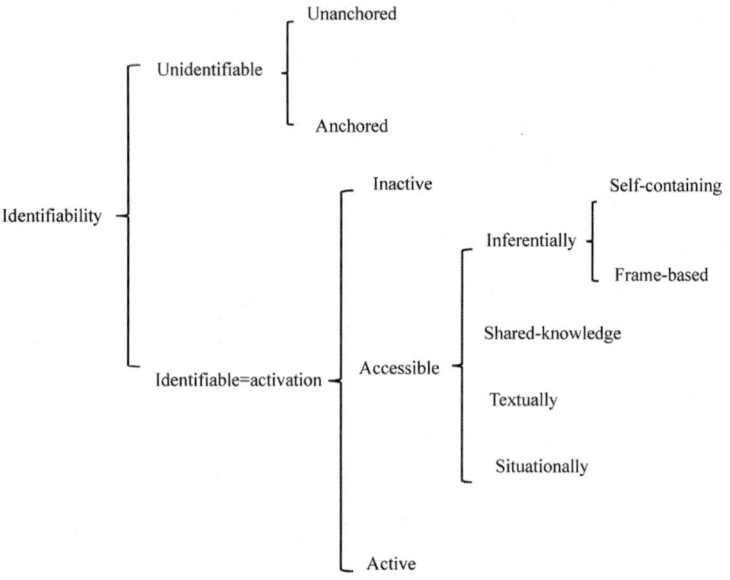

Figure 7-1 Model of identifiability

The nominal forms from focus and topic constituents of Chinese cleft data of the present study are checked from the perspective of their identifiability according to the context in which they are involved.

To provide a comprehensive perspective and assess the identifiability of focus and topic constituents separately, their distribution across various identifiable statuses is presented as follows (see Figure 7-2).

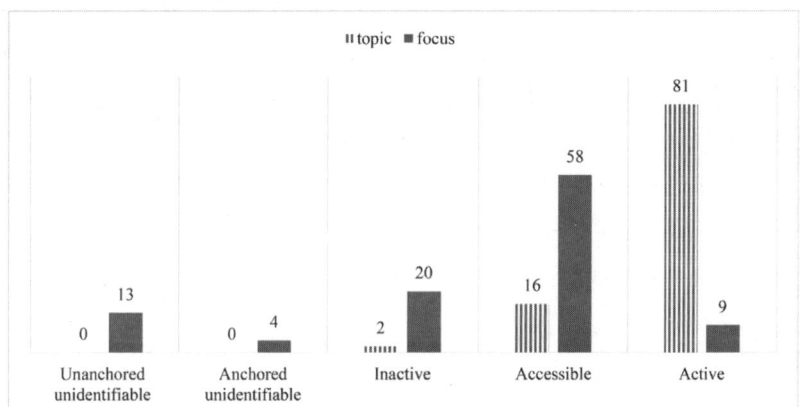

Figure 7-2 Identifiability of the focus and topic constituents in Chinese cleft sentences

All the possible identifiability of the focus and topic constituents of the tested examples show that the "unidentifiable unanchored" and "unidentifiable anchored" statuses are not eligible statuses for topic constituents of Chinese cleft sentences in the present study. However, the focus can be expressed in all of the five statuses of identifiability, and accessible status explains the identifiability of most of the focus cases. The detailed results are shown as follows.

(i) The topics in Chinese cleft sentences never represents unidentifiable references (unanchored or anchored) in Chinese cleft sentences.

(ii) This study's findings serve as evidence for the Topic Acceptability Scale proposed by Lambrecht (1994) (see Figure 4-2).

Active references are regularly put at the topic position of sentences, even in Chinese cleft sentences. In contrast, brand-new unanchored references are seldom used as topics due to their low acceptability at the topical position. The results of the present study re-examine the *Topic Acceptability Scale* as a universal and typological conclusion beyond the limitation of sentence structure and language differences.

(iii) No strict rules governing the identifiability or activation of focus constituents have been identified, as they are, in principle, not constrained by these factors. The constituent of the focus may be new or given information, but the relationship between the focus and the asserted proposition must be new[①]. Generally, there is no significant numerical distinction among the different categories of identifiability in the referents of focus constituents. However, slight variations among the four statuses can still be observed.

The following subsections provide a detailed analysis of argument-focus cleft sentences and adjunct-focus cleft sentences.

[①] The arguments about the newness and givenness of focus are mentioned and discussed in Chapter 6.

7.2 Identifiability of Focus and Topic Constituents in Argument-cleft Sentences

This section demonstrates the detailed identifiability of the focus and topic in argument and adjunct focus cleft sentences by examples.

(7-1) "别一个人到处乱跑,我还以为你给异鬼抓走了。" "他是被古灵精怪抓走的。"

Don't go around alone, I thought you had been captured by ghosts." "It was **the genie** who captured him. "

In the Chinese translation, " the genie" is a bare noun in Chinese whose definiteness is highly determined by its location and context. In this sentence, it is in contrast with the previous reference "ghosts". However, it refers to the general category of "the genie" rather than a specific instance. From the perspective of identifiability, it is unanchored unidentifiable with discourse-new and hearer-new information.

(7-2) ("我睡得很熟,"她带歉意地,) "你知道,我是眼用安眠药的。"

"I slept very deeply," she said apologetically. "You know, I take sleeping medications **by eyes**."

For most native speakers, "eye" is in focus with prosodic stress in this cleft sentence. Its focus position is apparent. Grammatically, it is a bare noun in Chinese, and the definiteness and identifiability of bare nouns are determined by locations and context. In this utterance, without any further explanation, hearers can easily interpret the reference of the bare noun "eye" as the eye of the speaker. Levinson's *I-principle* can be applied to explain this encoding procedure.

Levinson's *Information Principle* includes the *speaker's maxim—the maxim of minimization*, under which, the speaker may say as little as possible or provide only the minimum amount of linguistic information sufficient for communicative purposes; and *the recipient's corollary—the rule of en-*

richment. Under this maxim, the speaker amplifies the informational content of the speaker's utterance by finding the most specific interpretation, up to what you judge as the speaker's intended point. In example (7-2), from the speaker's side, she/he provides minimized information needed to understand the utterance based on his/her assumption towards the hearer. And the hearer should apply the rule of enrichment during the encoding procedure by establishing the conventional relationship between the event ("take sleeping meditations") and its object ("the person who takes sleeping meditations") referred to by the sentence. The underlying explanation for this reasoning procedure as well as the inferential identifiability is the fact that there are several unspoken *conventional relations* in people's memory stores, and they are self-explanatory, which means they can be made self-evident in a speech to comply with the "economic principle" of language use so that the speaker can "say as little as possible", and the listener can "expand" on this basis. The listener uses this as a basis for expanding the information content of the speaker's discourse. So, "eye" is discourse-new but hearer-old information for the current context, so it is an inactive reference.

(7-3) （1997年8月31日,戴安娜与男友多迪和一名司机一同死于巴黎车祸）多迪的父亲称,他的儿子和戴安娜是<u>**被英国特工害死的**</u>。

On August 31, 1997, Diana and her boyfriend Dodi, along with a driver, died in a car accident in Paris; However, Dodi's father claimed that <u>it was **the British agents** who killed his son and Diana</u>.

"The British agents" is a proper noun and it typically represents definiteness in Chinese.

(7-4) （如果我没记错的话,）昨天是<u>**你**为他提行李上楼的</u>。

If I remember correctly, <u>it was **you** who helped him carry the luggage upstairs</u>.

Grammatically, "you" is a pronoun; functionally, it is a deixis concerning the identification of the interlocutors or participant roles in the speech event. Second-person encodes the speaker's reference to certain (i.e., one or more) addresses through its participant role marked as [+Audience]. This deixis is active for the first party (speaker), the second party (audience), and the third party (other listeners), for it is discourse and hearer old.

To summarize, the identifiability of the focus constituent in argument-focus cleft sentences varied from unidentifiable to active, while the topics are mostly active and accessible.

To take argument-focus cleft sentences as examples, we can summarize that in Chinese cleft sentences, personal pronouns and the proper nouns deliver "active" or "accessible" status; the noun modified by the definite determiner (i.e., the Chinese demonstrative) has "active" status too. Bare nouns in focus show identifiable status expanding from identifiable to accessible and active. Through the above analysis of Chinese argument-focus cleft sentences, a connection has been established between Chen's (2004) research on definiteness in Chinese and the concept of identifiability within the framework of information structure.

7.3 Identifiability of Focus and Topic Constituents in Adjunct-cleft Sentences

The syntactic classes of the focus constituents in adjunct cleft sentences mainly include four types: VP, AdvP, PP, and NP. We are looking for the accessibility of the nominal phrases involved in these constituents, so all the nominal phrases are analyzed. This section demonstrates each identifiable category with examples.

7.3.1 Inferentially-accessible

The subcategories of "self-containing" and "frame-based" are merged into the category of "inferentially accessible", as shown in Figure 7-1.

(7-5) 陈存仪是**在抓住刘招华后的第一时间**由北京飞抵福建的。
Chen Cunyi flew back to Fujian from Beijing ***immediately after Liuzhaohua being caught***.

"Immediately after Liuzhaohua being caught" is the focus constituent of this cleft sentence. The head noun of this Chinese clause is actually "第一时间 (immediately after)", and "抓住刘招华 (Liuzhaohua being caught)" is the preceding modify- ing constituent linked to the head noun by the modifier "de". The focus is a self-contained one in which a constituent is evoked dependently of the other constituent.

(7-6) 继昨天进行两轮磋商之后,今天美方代表团三进三出中国外经贸部,最后的一次磋商是从下午三点四十分开始的,只进行了两小时二十分钟。
After two rounds of negotiation yesterday, the American delegation went to the Ministry of Commerce three times today. The last negotiation started **at *3.40 pm***, and it only lasted for 2 hours and 20 minutes.

The topic of the clause "the last negotiation" is a frame-based constituent that can be triggered by the previously mentioned constituent "two-round negotiations".

"Self-containing" and "frame-based" are two ways to realize the inferential accessibility; however, for simplicity and convenience, the "self-contained" reference and the "frame-based" reference are generally counted as "inferentially-accessible" ones. In other words, while this study employs the two concepts to assess "inferentially-accessible" references, it does not necessitate further categorization into "self-contained" or "frame-based" references.

(7-7) 此前，曾有接近米卢的人向我捎话，说"米卢准备和我谈一次"，但至今没有。我想，足球比赛是<u>用结果说明一切的</u>。
Previously, someone close to Milutinovic approached me and delivered a message, saying, " Milutinovic is preparing to have a conversation with me," but it hasn't happened yet. <u>I believe that in football competition, everything is explained **by *the results***</u>.

"The results" is discourse-new, however, it can be inferentially encoded by the hearer, for its association with the previously mentioned topic "football competition". In other words, "football competition" establishes a semantic frame involving "result" as one of the frame elements.

7.3.2 Inactive

(7-8) 他说,停火为伊拉克同西方建立新的关系铺平了道路。<u>阿拉法特是**由约旦**抵达这里访问的</u>。
He said that the ceasefire paved the way for Iraq to establish new relations with the West. <u>Arafat arrived here for a visit **from *Jordan***</u>.

"Jordan" is discourse-new for its first appearance into the discourse; however, it is hearer-old for staying in the long-term memory of the hearers of the current utterance.

(7-9) 泰国客人是<u>应中国人民外交学会的邀请</u>来访的。
The Thai guests visited China **at the invitation of** *the Chinese People's Institute of Foreign Affairs*.

In this example, "the Chinese People's Institute of Foreign Affairs" is a proper noun grammatically. It is discourse-new, but inactive reference for being stored in hearers' long-term memory at the moment of utterance.

7.3.3 Active

(7-10) 这让刘钟智又开始内疚,<u>是**他**让学习本来很好的儿子中途辍学回老家替自己赡养父母的</u>。
This made Liu Zhongzhi feel guilty again. <u>It was **he** who caused his son, who was originally doing well in his studies, to drop out midway and re- turn to their hometown to support his parents.</u>

" He" is anaphorically referred to by the previous proper name "(Liu Zhongzhi" . This anaphoric effect is intuitive and natural for native speakers

(7-11) 他和露西姑妈就是在那儿长大的,露西比她父亲大十五岁,他们的父母去世后,<u>是**她**一手把弟弟抚养大的</u>。
He and Aunt Lucy grew up there. Lucy is fifteen years older than her father. After their parents passed away, <u>it is **she** who raised her young brother all by herself.</u>

"She" is anaphorically linked to the previously mentioned proper name "Lucy". The use of the cleft construction "it is she who..." marks "she" not only as referentially identifiable, but also as discourse-prominent and active. This activates "Lucy" as a salient agent in the context, emphasizing her agency and responsibility in raising her younger brother. The shift from a descriptive clause to a cleft structure further foregrounds her subjecthood, reinforcing both emphasis and topic continuity.

7.3.4 Shared–knowledge accessible

(7-12) 不过,我们这一代知识分子,毕竟与我们的老师辈不太相同。<u>我们是**解放以后**成长起来的</u>。
However, we, the intellectuals of our generation, are quite different from our older generation of teachers. <u>We grew up after *the liberation*.</u>

"The liberation" is a proper noun known to all citizens of China for our mutual cultural background. So, despite its first appearance in the discourse, this proper noun shows shared-knowledge accessible status.

7.3.5 Situationally accessible

Most of the Chinese cleft sentences in this study put the time phrase as the focus of the sentence. Chen (2008) thought that time phrases in Chinese are situationally accessible. The followings are some examples.

(7-13) 6天之后，他携带着一大箱《伊利亚特》的各种译本，经法兰克福，换上了飞回祖国的班机……<u>他是5月10日回到祖国的</u>。

After six days, he carried a large box containing various translations of "The Iliad" and flew back to his homeland via Frankfurt... He returned to his homeland <u>on *May 10th*</u>.

(7-14) 李其炎市长一行是7日晚抵达此间进行访问的。

Mayor Li Qiyan and his delegation arrived here on the evening of the 7th for a visit.

"May 10th" and "the evening of the 7th" are time phrases that can be known or encoded by the hearer of the current utterance.

7.3.6 Unanchored unidentifiable

(7-15) 1989年凌叔华终于回到她热恋的故土，她是<u>让人抬着下飞机的</u>。

In 1989, Ling Shuhua finally returned to her beloved homeland. <u>She was carried off the plane **by *someone***</u>.

"Someone" here is a bare noun representing both a discourse-new and hearer-new information not anchored by other sentence constituents. It does not show the definiteness or specificity of the noun.

7.3.7 Anchored unidentifiable

(7-16) "哦,你们在那里呀! 我在监狱里找不到你,我还以为你已经逃了。" "是**我的一些部属**救我出来的。"
"Oh, there you are! I couldn't find you in prison, and I thought you had escaped." "It was *some of my subordinates* who rescued me"

"Some of my subordinates" is a possessive nominal phrase with the head being "some subordinates", and the modifier "my" is active for hearers, so it is anchored unidentifiable for the hearers.

7.4 Grammatical Expressions and Their Identifiability Status

The identifiability of the sentence constituent is a concept only relevant to nominal constituents; in this subsection, the grammatical expressions of these constituents are examined and the relationship between their grammatical classes and their statuses of identifiability is explored.

7.4.1 The word classes of topic and focus constituents

The syntactic categories of nominal phrases in the focus domain are already shown in Chapter 6. The results of the topic counterparts are shown in Figure 7-3.

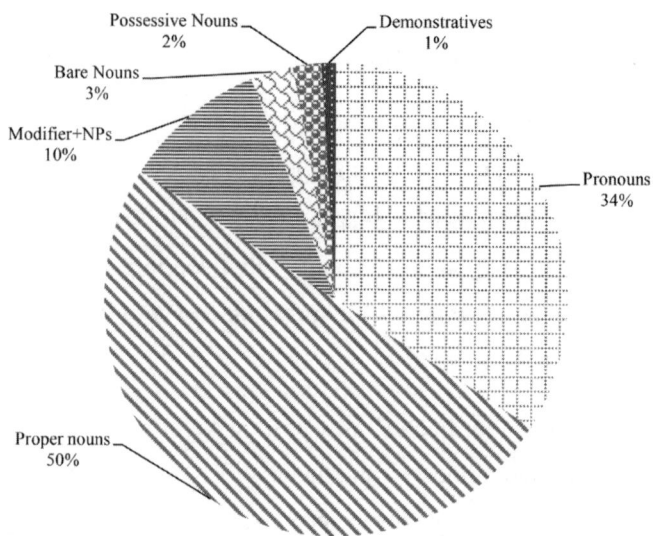

Figure 7-3 The syntactic categories of topic constituents of Chinese cleft sentences

In most instances, one topic is associated with one focus. All topic and focus constituents are checked in accordance with their word classes. By doing that, the result shows the correlation between certain specific word classes (e.g., bare nouns) and their informative roles (i.e., focus/topic).

As previously noted, the ideal scenario entails a one-to-one correspondence between the topic and focus in each cleft sentence. However, in the present study, the total number of topic constituents differs from that of focus constituents. The numerical discrepancy can be attributed to two factors: first, the presence of empty topics in the data; second, the occurrence of topical focus. The concept of "topical focus" was proposed by Xu and Liu (1998) after they found out that specific constituents possess a topic nature and a contrastive function simultaneously. They have identified the characteristics of such elements, but due to adhering to the defining feature of "contrastivity" as the focus, they have found a compromise and termed it the "topical focus" even if they admitted that: "The possibility of the topic serving as a contrasting focus is not close to zero, but truly zero" (1998, p.101). In other words, topic and focus are incompatible. If "contrastivity" is not regarded as the defining

Chapter 7　The Identifiability of the Focus and Topic Constituents in Chinese Cleft Sentences

characteristic of focus but rather as an independent functional feature that can be associated with both the topic and focus components, then this issue can be easily resolved. Zhou (2009), therefore, treated the "topical focus" concept as a contrastive topic instead of a focus in nature. The following two examples, drawn from his study, illustrate the distinction between contrastive focus and contrastive topic (i.e., topical focus in Xu and Liu's terminology).

(7-17)　A: 老王当过海军。
　　　　B: 老张当过海军。
　　　　B': (不对, 是) 老张。
　　　　A: Lao Wang served in the Navy.
　　　　B: Lao Zhang served in the Navy.
　　　　B': (No), (it is) Lao Zhang.

(7-18)　A: 老王当过空军。
　　　　B: 老张, 当过海军。
　　　　B': *(不对, 是) 老张。
　　　　A: Lao Wang served in the air force.
　　　　B: Lao Zhang served in the Navy.
　　　　B': * Lao Zhang.

In contrastive focus sentences, elements outside the focus can be omitted because the contrast is entirely carried by the specified focus element. The listener is expected to infer the omitted information from the context, as the contrast between alternatives is clear. However, in topical focus sentences, the emphasis lies on the entire statement following the topic. In these sentences, every element outside the topic is essential to convey the full, new information. If these elements are omitted, the listener loses critical context, and the intended meaning cannot be fully recovered.

Applying this to the ungrammatical behavior observed in the example (7-18) — where the response omits parts of the statement — the omission blurs the intended information. This incomplete response violates the requirement of topical focus that demands the preservation of all information following the topic. Hence, the omission, which is acceptable in contrastive focus, leads to ungrammaticality when a topical focus is expected. This difference in omission rules is one method to distinguish between topical and contrastive focus constructions

Let us test this method with one example collected from the present study.

(7-19) 他₁①和露西姑妈₂就是在那儿长大的,露西₂比她₃父亲₁大十五岁,他们₁₊₂的父母去世后,<u>是**她**₂一手把弟弟₁抚养大的</u>。

He and Aunt Lucy grew up there. Lucy is fifteen years older than her father. After their parents passed away, <u>it is **she** who raised her young brother all by herself.</u>

"She" in this sentence is treated as the topical focus instead of contrastive focus, and it is clear that "she" form the topic chain for the present study. However, if we apply the test proposed by Zhou (2009) by omitting the elements besides focus, the sentence is ungrammatical.

(7-20) *他₁和露西姑妈₂就是在那儿长大的,露西₂比她₃父亲₁大十五岁,他们₁₊₂的父母去世后,<u>是她</u>。

* He and Aunt Lucy grew up there. Lucy is fifteen years older than her father. After their parents passed away, <u>it is she</u>.

According to Zhou's interpretation, the acceptability of omitting elements other than the focus stems from the fact that "topical focus" functions as the topic rather than the focus of the sentence. In sentences containing a topical focus, the focal emphasis is placed on constituents other than the topic itself. The omission of these elements results in the ungrammaticality of the

---

① The numbered footnotes "1" "2" and "3" show the referring relationship between different nominal phrases. Nominal phrases with the same footnotes are co-referential.

sentence, as exemplified in (7-20). This observation supports the claim that "she" in (7-19) does not serve as a contrastive focus but rather as the topical focus of the sentence.

A closer examination of the cleft sentence "It is she who single-handedly raised her young brother" reveals that this construction — [SHI + subject + adverbial + BA + object + VP + DE] — lacks a topic preceding the focus marker "shi". Structurally, [subject + adverbial + BA + object + VP] constitutes a complete canonical sentence in Chinese, where "she" serves as the topic. In the canonical sentence "She raised her young brother all by herself", "she' clearly functions as the topic. However, due to the syntactic positioning of the canonical sentence within the cleft construction and the focalizing role of "shi', it cannot be considered the topic of sentence (7-19). Instead, in the cleft structure, "she" acts as the topical focus, serving as a crucial referential anchor within the topic chain of the matrix sentence.[①]

Let us come back to the grammatical categories of topic and focus constituents.

The Figure 7-4 shows that proper nouns are commonly used as both the topic and focus in Chinese cleft sentences. Pronouns, on the other hand, are more frequently employed as the topic rather than the focus. Modifier+noun combinations and bare nouns tend to function predominantly as the focus rather than as the topic within discourse. At the same time, this study does include instances of reflexive pronouns and demonstrative+nouns, although they are relatively infrequent. Figure 7-4 summarizes the distribution of nominal phrase types within the domains of focus and topic.

[①] Chinese cleft sentences with contrastive focus and topical focus express different functions. The functions of Chinese cleft sentences are further categorized into contrastive, topical, and informational functions, based on different semantic and pragmatic properties.

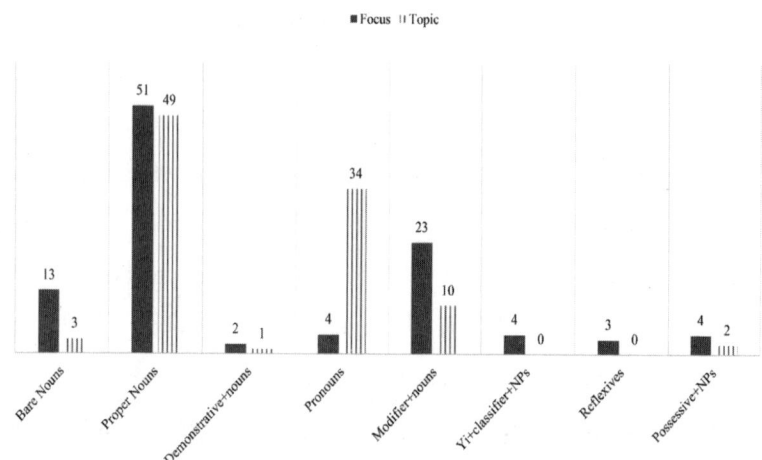

Figure 7-4 Word classes vs. the focus/topic nominal constituents

According to Chen (2004), definite, indefinite and indeterminate expressions in Chinese are varied in degrees of identifiability. In Chinese, there are some grammatical means to express definite and indefinite, even if there are no articles, which are the most unmarked way to express definiteness in languages such as English. The definiteness of Chinese is not grammaticalized as English grammar does, and it is widely accepted that it is limited more by pragmatic factors than grammatical ones.

In the next section, the degrees of identifiability expressed by the above word classes in the collected sentences are examined.

7.4.2 The degrees of identifiability of different word classes

Ariel (1990) held the idea that, among Chinese proper nouns, pronouns, and nouns modified by definite determiners, the reference of a pronoun normally registers a higher degree of identifiability than that of the other two types (cf. Ariel, 1990). This postulation is examined through the data collected in the present study.

Chapter 7 The Identifiability of the Focus and Topic Constituents in Chinese Cleft Sentences

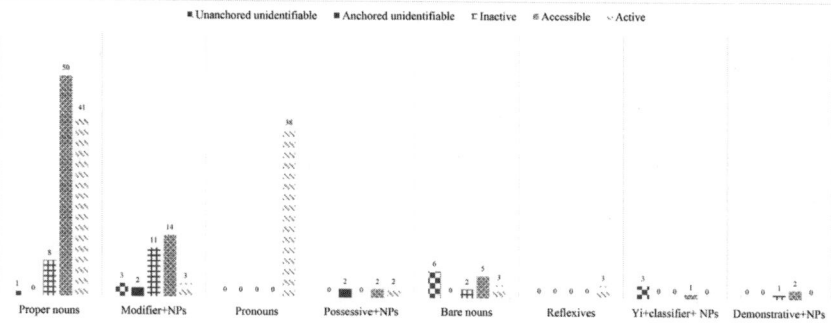

Figure 7-5 Word classes and identifiability

In analyzing the relationship between identifiability types and word classes, this study does not differentiate among the specific subtypes of accessibility. Instead, the four subcategories — inferentially accessible, shared knowledge-accessible, textually accessible, and situationally accessible — are integrated into a single overarching category: accessible. This classification facilitates the establishment of a hierarchical continuum alongside the other three categories: unidentifiable, inactive, and active, providing a more systematic framework for analysis.

Figure 7-5 illustrates the relationship between lexical categories and identifiability. Based on the present study's data, pronouns exclusively express the active status of reference. Most proper nouns denote active and accessible references. Modifier+nouns have a relatively balanced distribution ranging from unanchored unidentifiable to active, although among them, accessible and inactive are the two types with the highest frequency. Bare nouns express unanchored identifiable, inactive, accessible, and active references. "Yi+classifier+nouns" are known as indefinite expressions in Chinese. In this present study, three cases exhibit the unanchored unidentifiable reference, while one case shows the accessible references. Demonstrative+nouns are widely accepted as Chinese definite markers. In this study, only three cases were identified: one is classified as an inactive reference, while the other two are categorized as accessible references.

The "active" and "accessible" data outnumber the other three categories. Two types of syntactic classes mainly express the activeness of the reference — proper nouns and pronouns.

A mere examination of the distribution of each word class across the four identifiability statuses is insufficient to determine the precise degree of identifiability for each word class in the focus/topic positions of Chinese cleft sentences. To quantify and compare the degrees of identifiability of these grammatical expressions, a numerical scale is assigned to each identifiability status, reflecting variations in identifiability among referents represented by different grammatical forms.

A five-point scale is used to represent different levels of identifiability. "Unanchored unidentifiable" references receive a score of 1, indicating the lowest degree of identifiability, while "anchored identifiable" references are assigned a score of 2. "Inactive" references receive a score of 3, whereas "accessible" references are assigned a score of 4. Finally, "active" references receive the highest score of 5, representing the strongest degree of identifiability.

Given the varying total frequencies of different word classes, the analysis focuses on the proportion of each word class within the unidentifiable, inactive, accessible, and active categories. These proportions serve as the basis for calculating the degree of identifiability, as illustrated in the Figure 7-6.

The types with the highest degree of identifiability of references are pronouns and reflexives. And proper nouns hold the second place. The identifiability of demonstrative NPs and possessive NPs exhibits a comparable level of identifiability, and modifier+NPs have a closely aligned level of identifiability. The "yi+classifier+noun" shows the lowest identifiability. This calculation partially agrees with Ariel's (1990) findings, indicating that proper nouns and the pronouns high degrees of identifiability.

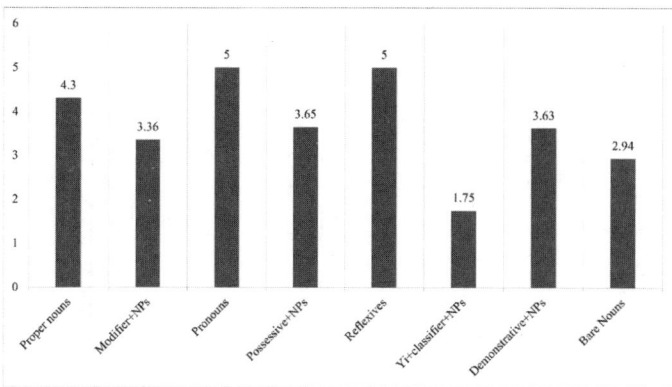

Figure 7-6 Degrees of identifiability of references represented by different grammatical expressions

In line with Chen's speculation of the definiteness tendency of Chinese nouns, this result shows a similar relationship between Chinese nouns and identifiability. Proper names, personal pronouns, demonstrative and possessive NPs show a relatively high degree of identifiability. "Yi+classifer" is considered the most important indefinite determiner in Chen's study. The "Yi+classifier+nouns" expression aims to denote the generality instead of the definiteness of the reference. Unlike the other numerals, "yi" with a classifier has undergone a process of grammaticalization to become a marker of indefiniteness, similar to how the English indefinite article "a" evolved from the numeral "one." Apart from being used as a pronoun and determiner, "yi" with a classifier performs all the essential functions of a regular indefinite article like "a" in English. The result of this study proves its low degree of identifiability.

Bare nouns are indeterminate representations of definiteness in Chinese, as shown by the above graph, the identifiability is about the middle level.

The ranking of the identifiability of the word classes for the topic and focus constituents is show by Figure 7-7.

The following examples are provided to illustrate the informative and syntactic configurations of Chinese cleft sentences.

Figure 7-7　Ranking of the identifiability of different syntactic categories

(7-21)　我前天看了是《珍珠衫》嘀,评剧嘀,<u>当时呢</u>[②] 我们是**晚**上看**的**。

I watched *Pear Liner* the day before yesterday. It is a Pingju. We watched it **at night**.

Table 7-1　Demonstration of examples from the perspectives of information, syntactic structures, word classes, identifiability, and thematic roles (example 7-21)

Sentence	当时我们 At that time, we.	是 SHI$_{aux}$	晚上 at night	看 watched	的 De$_{ptcl}$
Information structure	Topic	–	Focus	–	–
	Presupposition$_i$	–	Focus	Presupposition$_i$	–
	Assertion				–
Syntactic structures	Subject	–	Adjunct	verb	–
Syntactic categories	Personal pronoun	Auxiliary	Bare Noun	verb	Particle
Identifiability	Active	–	Inferential accessible	–	–

The focus expresses the inactiveness of its reference by the grammatical form of a bare noun. On the one hand, it is discourse-new; on the other hand,

---

[①]　A detailed analysis of the information structure, syntactic structure, syntactic category and identifiability status of sentence (7-20) are elaborated in Table 7-1.

[②]　The particle "呢 (ne)" functions as a mood marker, indicating a pause in an utterance. It does not carry any syntactic or informational significance and is therefore omitted from the table(7-1) for simplicity.

the reference of the time "night" is not explicitly expressed but inferentially evoked by the hearer. The topic is the subject of the sentence whose meaning is actively referential to the hearer.

(7-22)　继昨天进行两轮磋商之后,今天美方代表团三进三出中国外经贸部,<u>最后的一次磋商是从下午三点四十分开始的</u>,只进行了两小时二十分钟。

After the two rounds of negotiations yesterday, American representatives went to MOFTEC three times today. <u>The last negotiation started **from 3:40 pm** and only lasted for 2 hours and 20 minutes.</u>

Table 7-2 presents a detailed analysis.

Table 7-2　Demonstration of examples from the perspectives of information, syntactic structures, word classes, identifiability, and thematic (example 7-22)

Sentence	最后的一次磋商 the last negation)	是 SHI$_{aux}$	从下午三点四十分 from 3.40 pm	开始 start	的 DE$_{ptcl}$
Information structure	Topic	–	Focus	–	–
	Presupposition$_i$	–	Focus	Presupposition$_i$	–
	\multicolumn{4}{c}{Assertion}		–
Syntactic structures	Subject	–	Adjunct	Verb	–
Syntactic categories	Modified noun	Auxiliary	Prepositional phrase (preposition+bare noun)	Verb	Particle
Identifiability	Inferentially accessible	–	Situationally accessible	–	–

Between the communicators, the temporal reference remains accessible due to their shared knowledge. Although "negotiation" was previously mentioned, the modifiers preceding it differ, making the two noun phrases non-identical. Instead, the second instance is inferentially retrievable by the hearer.

To understand this inferential reasoning, we can draw on Du Bois' (1980) explanation of three conditions under which English definites are introduced early in discourse.

(i) those marked by an unstressed demonstrative.

(ii) those containing identifying information within a postmodifying relative clause, and.

(iii) those established through association with a cognitive frame.

Additionally, noun phrases (NPs) that convey specific and new information within the presupposed structure of a restrictive relative clause may also render a definite initial mention acceptable. As Du Bois (1980, p. 222) illustrated with the example "she knocks the hat that he's wearing off on the ground," the identifying information provided by defining relative clauses can justify the use of a definite article for the entire NP, and vice versa.

Regarding the third type, Du Bois (1980) posited that a larger whole or a specific activity can function as a frame, enabling the definite initial mention of references typically associated with them. Examples include "the living room – the wall" (Du Bois 1980, p. 233) and "sell – the money" (Du Bois 1980, p. 215).

In the case of (7-22), "the last negotiation" is a modified nominal phrase, consisting of the modifier " 的 (de)" and the nominal head "negotiation", which serves as an active reference. According to Du Bois (1980), the modified nominal phrase exhibits partial inferentiality, with the nominal head playing a crucial role in its interpretation

(7-23) 我在那儿住了十几年了,搬到东城区又十几年了,我是七一年退休的,七一年从干校回来的。

I lived there for more than 10 years and moved to Dongcheng District and lived there for more than another 10 years. I retired

in 1971, and I was back from the cadre school in 1971.

Please see the detailed analysis in Table 7-3.

Table 7-3 Demonstration of examples from the perspectives of information, syntactic structures, word classes, identifiability, and thematic roles (example 7-23)

Sentence		我 I	是 SHI$_{aux}$	七一年 YEAR 1971	退休 retired	的 DE$_{ptcl}$
Information structure		Topic	–	Focus	–	–
		Presupposition$_i$	–	Focus	Presupposition$_i$	–
		Assertion				–
Syntactic structures		Subject	–	Adjunct	Verb	–
Syntactic categories		Personal pronoun	Auxiliary	Proper nouns	Verb	Particle
Identifiability		Active	–	Situationally accessible	–	–

The topic constituent is active and the as most of the time phrases, this focus constituent is situationally accessible from the perspective of identifiability.

7.5　The Markedness of Chinese Cleft Sentences from the Perspective of Focus Typology

Building on the Prague School's work on communicative dynamism (e.g., Firbas, 1966; Mathesius, 1929), the late 1990s saw a growing interest in classifying how languages grammatically structure the expression of different information statuses assigned to sentence elements. In other words, this research focused on the typological differences among languages with respect to focus structure.

According to Van Valin (1999), languages can be distinguished based on: whether they exhibit rigid focus structure: "languages in which the potential focus domain is the entire main clause in simple sentences will be considered to have flexible focus structure, whereas those in which the potential focus domain is restricted to a subpart of the main clause will be considered to have rigid focus structure" (Van Valin, 1999, pp, 3-4).

From a general point of view, Chinese is a language with a flexible focus structure, in which the potential focus domain should be any constituent or the whole main clause of a simple sentence.

For example, in the following "shi ... de" sentences, the focus falls on different constituents ranging from the whole VP or the whole clause to the subject, or the direct NP alone.

(7-24) 我是**该走了**。

Wǒ shì gāi zǒu le.

1SG SHI$_{aux}$ have to leave LE$_{aspc}$.

I have to leave indeed.

(7-24) is an emphatic sentence in which the focus domain encompasses the whole sentence.

(7-25) 我是**昨天**到北京的。

Wǒ shì zuótiān dào Běijīng de.

1SG SHI$_{aux}$ yesterday arrive Beijing DE$_{ptcl}$.

It was **yesterday** that I arrived in Beijing.

(7-26) 苹果**在桌上**。

Píngguǒ zài zhuō shàng.

Apple on table.

The apple **is on the table**.

(7-26) is a topicalized sentence in which the focus domain falls on the prepositional predicate.

(7-27) 桌子上**有苹果**。

Zhuōzi shàng yǒu píngguǒ.

Table on have apple.

There is an apple on the table.

(7-27) is an existential sentence in which the focus domain falls on the complement.

(7-28) 我捡起来的是**钢笔**。
Wǒ jiǎn qǐlái de shì gāngbǐ.
1SG pick up DE$_{rel}$ SHI$_{cop}$ pen.
What I picked up is **a pen**.

(7-28) is a pseudo-cleft sentence in which the focus domain falls on the object.

(7-29) 为了这次约会，我甚至**去买了皮鞋**。
Wèile zhè cì yuēhuì, wǒ shènzhì qù mǎi le píxié.
For this-CL date, 1SG even go buy LE$_{aspc}$ leather shoes.
For this date, I even **went to buy leather shoes**.

(7-29) is a contrast clause in which the focus domain is the verb phrase (VP).

We can reasonably assume that Chinese exhibits a flexible focus structure, while cleft sentences — similar to topicalized sentences, existential sentences, emphatic sentences, pseudo-cleft sentences, and contrast clauses — are all marked constructions.

7.6 Summary

Considering the relationship between topic/focus and identifiability, the following conclusions can be drawn.

(i) In Chinese cleft sentences, the topic is never an unidentifiable reference, whether unanchored or anchored.

(ii) The identifiability of topic constituents in Chinese cleft sentences aligns with and provides empirical support for the Topic Acceptability Scale proposed by Lambrecht (1994).

The detailed acceptability of the criteria see Figure 7-8.

Figure 7-8 The degree of acceptance of the identifiable status for topic constituents in Chinese cleft sentences

Active references are regularly put at the topic position of sentences, even in Chinese cleft sentences. In contrast, unidentifiable references are seldom used as a topic due to their low acceptability at the topical position. The findings of this study reassess the *Topic Acceptability Scale* as a universal and typological principle, extending beyond the constraints of sentence structure and cross-linguistic variation.

(iii) The focused constituent can represent either new or known information, but it must establish a new connection (or new message coined by Chu (2018)) with the asserted proposition. In summary, there is no significant numerical difference among the various identifiability categories of focus constituents, although minor distinctions exist across the four statuses.

Most of the nominal focus constituents in cleft sentences of this study fall into the active and accessible identifiable types, surpassing the other three. Considering the syntactic categories of the focused constituents of Chinese cleft sentences, pronouns mainly indicate the active state of the reference. Most proper nouns represent references that are both active and accessible. Regarding modifier+nouns, their distribution ranges from unanchored and unidentifiable to active, with accessible and inactive being the most frequently observed types. Bare nouns with limited data can express references that are unanchored identifiable, inactive, accessible, or active. Demonstrative+nouns in the present study are interpreted as inactive and accessible references. "Yi+classifier+nouns" in this study indicate unanchored unidentifiable and accessible reference.

By checking the degrees of identifiability presented by different syntactic categories, we draw a similar conclusion to Chen's speculation of the definiteness tendency of Chinese nouns. The ranking of the identifiability of the word classes for the topic and focus constituents is shown by Figure 7-7.

Considering the relationship between the degree of identifiability and the word classes, the present study partially proves the conclusion proposed by Ariel (1990) that pronouns have a higher degree of identifiability than other word classes. Besides the three categories mentioned by Ariel (1990), shown by the present study, modifier+nouns and possessive+nouns exhibit relatively high and similar degree of identifiability. Bare nouns present relatively low degree of identifiability, and "yi+classifier+NPs" show the lowest degree of identifiability.

Finally, from a focus typological point of view, Chinese cleft sentences are considered marked constructions of Chinese that hold rigid focus structures.

Chapter 8

Conclusion

This book provides a comprehensive examination of cleft sentences in Chinese, addressing several key issues. It explores the distinctive features of Chinese cleft constructions and their differences from other "shi ... de" sentences from the perspective of information structure. Additionally, it analyzes the grammatical and informational interpretations of cleft focus in Chinese cleft sentences and investigates the identifiability of focus and topic in relation to information distribution.

Based on empirical data collected and organized from two corpora, all qualifying instances are further analyzed in terms of their semantic and pragmatic interpretations, as well as their information structure configuration. The conclusions are stated in the following sections.

8.1 Chinese Cleft Sentences and Chinese "shi⋯de" Sentences

Semantic, pragmatic and informative properties of cleft sentences are treated as the criteria of Chinese cleft sentences to distinguish cleft sentences from other "shi ... de" sentences. The followings are some tentative answers for the hypothesis proposed in Chapter 1.

(i) As with most general sentences, there is a bipartition of "presupposition" and " focus" in Chinese cleft sentences; however, the configuration and the properties of the presupposition and focus differ from other "shi...de" sentences. Firstly, the presupposition of Chinese cleft sentences takes the form of an open proposition, though the specific structure varies slightly between argument-focus and adjunct-focus cleft sentences. Fundamentally, this presupposition is existential in nature. Secondly, the presupposition and the focus are not partitioned in a clear-demarcated way. Finally, "shi" and "de" are not involved in the presupposition or the focus.

The nature of the presupposition of Chinese cleft sentences is existential in both argument-focus and adjunct-focus cleft sentences. Unlike argument-focus cleft sentences, the presuppositions of adjunct cleft sentences are "event-existential presuppositions". The argument-focus clefts exhibit an existential presupposition constituted by a "有 (have)" proposition inferred from the listener. In contrast, the event-existential presupposition shows the existence of action through a proposition in which the focus constituent is replaced by its hypernym, defining the semantic set presupposed by the sentence.

(ii) The focus constituent exhibits exhaustivity. Exhaustivity is an essential feature in distinguishing Chinese cleft sentences from other "shi … de" sentences, such as "shi … de" copula and emphatic sentences.

Following these criteria, Chinese "shi … de" clefts cannot be classified as a subcategory of Chinese "shi" copula sentences and thus makes the word class of "shi" and "de" different from those in copula sentences. Based on the data from this study, Chinese "shi … de" sentences are classified according to semantic function, presupposition, the word class of "shi", the word class of "de", and exhaustivity. As a result, they are categorized into equational, attributive, existential, emphatic and cleft sentences.

By examining the relationship between the argument and predicate as well as instances where "shi" and "de" are omitted, this study concludes that in Chinese cleft sentences, "shi" functions as a raising auxiliary, allowing subject-auxiliary inversion, while "de" serves as a parasitic category that acts as a mood particle, reinforcing the confirmative and assertive tone and enhancing the evidentiality of the existential presupposition. Additionally, under certain conditions (though not necessarily in all cases), "de" also encodes tense/aspect information within the sentence.

In Chinese cleft constructions, "shi" can generally be omitted. However, if "de" conveys tense/aspect distinctions, particularly indicating past tense or past perfect aspect, it cannot be omitted.

8.2 Types of Chinese Cleft Sentences and the Grammatical Categories of Focus/Topic Constituents

Concerning the second hypothesis, this study concludes, from the empirical data, that VPs can be focused in Chinese (being the adjunct of the sentence). And among all the syntactic categories of focus constituents (i.e., AP, AdvP, NP, PP, VP), PPs takes the prominent position with the highest frequency of occurrence.

This finding contradicts the third hypothesis, as observational data reveal numerous instances of adjunct-focus cleft sentences. At least within the present corpus, argument-focus cleft sentences are relatively scarce. In contrast, adjunct-focus cleft sentences occur more frequently, with the focus primarily serving to describe, modify, or explain various aspects of the action expressed in the sentence.

The differences between argument-focus cleft sentences and adjunct-focus cleft sentences primarily lie in two key aspects: distinct focus domains and different presuppositional configurations. In argument-focus cleft sentences, the presupposition is existential, whereas in adjunct-focus cleft sentences, the presupposition pertains to event-existentiality.

Regarding the grammatical categories of focus domains of Chinese cleft sentences, prepositional phrases constitute the largest proportion, followed by nominal phrases, with verb phrases ranking third, and adjective phrases coming last. Among all the grammatical categories of the nominal phrases of focus constituents, proper nouns rank first, then come modifier+nouns and bare nouns.

By analyzing the definiteness of noun phrases (NPs) within the focus domain of cleft sentences in this research, we deduced that the definiteness of Chinese NPs is not directly linked to focus. In other words, the focus of Chinese cleft sentences does not exhibit a preference for either definite or indefinite NPs. In Chinese cleft sentences, focus constituents have a strong tendency towards new information/ message, instead of indefiniteness.

8.3 Identifiability of Focus and Topic Constituents

The identifiability of topic constituents of Chinese cleft sentences re-examines the *Topic Acceptability Scale* proposed by Lambrecht (1994); however, the results did not deduce identifiable scale for focus constituents.

Considering the identifiable degrees of different grammatical categories, this study draws a similar conclusion as Chen's proposal of the definiteness tendency of Chinese nouns and Ariel's (1990) conclusion of degrees of identifiability of different word classes.

8.4 Theoretical and Practical Contribution

This book offers the first comprehensive study of Chinese cleft sentences, integrating insights from syntax, semantics, pragmatics, and information structure. It systematically identifies the defining criteria that set Chinese cleft constructions apart from other "shi...de" sentences.

The criteria avoid the typological confusion caused by directly applying the criteria of English cleft sentences to the Chinese counterparts by the method of translation; at the same time, the criteria support the suggestions of analyzing Chinese grammar from an informative point of view, as advocated by many Chinese scholars. I believe that these criteria provide a new framework for identifying Chinese cleft sentences, helping to clarify ambiguities stemming from misinterpretations in previous studies, such as the confusion between cleft and "shi" copula sentences. Additionally, these criteria offer cross-linguistic applicability, serving as a general diagnostic tool for cleft constructions in languages like Chinese, where traditional syntactic criteria may be less effective.

As far as can be determined, this study appears to be among the first attempts to classify Chinese cleft sentences according to focus structure and to investigate their usage patterns through corpus data. The findings categorize Chinese cleft sentences into argument-focus and adjunct-focus types, with adjunct-focus cleft sentences occurring more frequently than argument-focus cleft sentences.

By examining the relationships among focus, topic, identifiability, and new/given information, this study provides empirical support for Lambrecht's (1994) Topic Accessibility Scale and Ariel's (1990) identifiability hierarchy. The findings align with the information-structure approach to Chinese grammar, demonstrating that definiteness/identifiability, new/given information, and focus/topic do not have a one-to-one correspondence.

As an interdisciplinary study, this research aims to contribute to both theoretical linguistics and Chinese language pedagogy. Its findings — including the defining criteria for Chinese cleft sentences, the correlation between information structure and cognitive identifiability, and the role of syntactic definiteness — offer valuable insights for further linguistic analysis and language teaching practices.

8.5   Limitations and Future Research Directions

Further investigation, particularly with additional data on cleft sentences containing bare "shi" and "de", would offer a more nuanced understanding of structural variations within Chinese cleft sentences. Although, the total number of qualifying instances in the present study remains limited, access to a larger empirical dataset could enable a more refined classification of "shi … de" sentences, allowing for deeper exploration of the syntactic properties of focus constituents and a more comprehensive account of the conditions governing the omission of "shi" and "de".

As key parameters of information structure, phonological factors will be considered in future research. Given that this study primarily examines information structure through the syntactic configuration of Chinese cleft sentences, phonological aspects have been excluded. Future studies will investigate phonological parameters, provided that advanced scientific equipment and sufficient empirical data are available.

From a pedagogical perspective, assessing the applicability of this study's findings in Chinese as a Second Language classrooms for non-native speakers would be both practical and meaningful. Further empirical studies in this area are highly encouraged.

References

曹道根,包琳玲."的"的语气词归属问题和汉语分裂句的传信功能[J].中国语言学报,2018(18):32-51.

曹道根.事物化和事态——再论自指和转指[J].中国语文,2019(4):430-446.

陈平.汉语的形式、意义与功能[M].北京:商务印书馆,2017.

丁玲.莎菲女士的日记[M].南京:江苏文艺出版社,2008。

邓守信.有关汉语分裂句的一些问题.中国语言学报[J],1979:101-114.

方梅.汉语对比焦点的句法表现手段[J].中国语文,1995(4):279-288.

刘丹青,徐烈炯.焦点与背景,话题及汉语"连"字句[J].中国语文.1998(4):243-252.

刘月华.实用现代汉语语法[M].北京:商务印刷出版社,1983.

刘莹,李宝伦.穷尽性还是对比性?——从英语分裂句看汉语焦点类"是"字句的语义[J].外语教学与研究.2019,51(5):677-688+799.

刘莹,程工.从焦点的类型看"的"字结构的语义[J].中国语文,2021(1):28-42.

陆俭明.再谈语言信息结构理论[J].外语教学与研究,2018(2):163-172.

吕叔湘.中国文法要略中卷[M].北京:商务印书出版社,1944.

吕叔湘.现代汉语八百词[M].北京:商务印书出版社,1980.

屈承熹.信息结构的基本概念及其在现代汉语中的表达形式[J].汉

语学习, 2018（2）: 3-14.

屈承熹. 语言学论集: 理论、应用及汉语法 [M]. 台北: 文鹤出版社, 1979.

沈家煊. 汉语有没有"主谓结构" [J]. 现代外语, 2017 40（1）: 1-13.

石毓智. 论判断、焦点、强调与对比之关系——"是"的语法功能和使用条件 [J]. 语言研究, 2005（4）: 43-53.

宋玉柱. 关于"是……的"结构的分析 [J]. 天津师范大学学报, 1978（4）: 75-76.

宋玉柱. 关于"把"字句的两个问题 [J]. 语文研究, 1981（2）: 39-43.

汤廷池. 国语的焦点结构: 分裂句分裂变句准分裂句. 汉语句法语意论集 [C]. 台北: 台北学生书局, 1983: 127-226.

王红旗. "把"字句的意义究竟是什么？ [J]. 语文研究, 2003（87）: 35-40.

王力. 中国语法理论: 上 [M]. 上海: 中华书局, 1944.

徐杰, 李英哲. 焦点和两个非线性语法范畴: "否定""疑问" [J]. 中国语文, 1993（2）: 81-102.

徐烈炯, 刘丹青. 话题的结构与功能 [M]. 上海: 上海教育出版社, 1998.

袁毓林. 从焦点理论看句尾"的"的句法语义功能 [J]. 中国语文, 2003（1）: 3-16.

张伯江, 方梅. 汉语功能语法研究 [M]. 南昌: 江西教育出版社, 1996.

赵元任, 吕叔湘. 汉语口语语法 [M]. 北京: 商务印刷出版社, 1979.

周立波. 暴风骤雨 [M]. 北京: 人民文学出版社, 2009.

周韧. 什么样的"客人"来了？ [J]. 语言教学与研究, 2020（2）: 51-63.

周士宏. 从信息结构角度看焦点结构的分类 [J]. 汉语学习, 2008（5）: 35-42.

周士宏. 信息结构中的对比焦点和对比话题——兼论话题焦点的性质 [J]. 解放军外国语学院学报, 2009（4）: 12-16.

朱德熙. "的"字结构和判断句 [J]. 中国语文, 1978（1）: 23-27.

朱德熙. 说"的". 现代汉语语法研究 [M]. 北京: 商务出版社, 1980.

宗成庆, 吴华, 黄泰翼, 等. 限定领域汉语口语对话语料分析 [C]. 全国第五届计算语言联合学术会议论文集, 1999: 115-122.

Abrusán M. Presupposition cancellation: Explaining the 'soft-hard' trigger distinction [J]. Natural Language Semantics, 2016 (24): 165-202.

Ahlemeyer B, and Kohlhof, I. Bridging the Cleft: An Analysis of the Translation of English it-clefts into German [J]. Languages in Contrast, 1999,2 (1): 1-25.

Akmajian A. On deriving cleft sentences from pseudo-cleft sentences [J]. Linguistic Inquiry, 1970, 1(2):149-168.

Aijmer K, Altenberg B. Johansson M. Languages in contrast: Papers from a symposium on text-based cross-linguistic studies, Lund 4-5 March 1994 [M]. Lund studies in English, 1996.

Ammann H. Die menschliche Rede. Sprachphilosophische Untersuchungen [M]. Wissenschaftliche Buchgesellschaft, 1925.

Altmann H. Cleft- und Pseudocleft-Sätze (Spalt- und Sperrsätze) im Deutschen [J]. An der Grenze zwischen Grammatik und Pragmatik, 2009: 13–34.

Ariel M. Accessing noun phrase antecedents[M]. London: Routledge, 1990.

Atlas J. D. and Levinson S C. It-clefts, informativeness and logical form: Radical pragmatics (revised standard version) [M]// Radical Pragmatics. Academic Press. 1981: 1-62.

Badan L, F Del Gobbo. On the syntax of topic and focus in Chinese [M]// Beninca P. Munaro N. Mapping the Left Periphery. New York: Oxford University Press, 2011: 63-90.

Ball C N. Th-clefts [J]. Pennsylvania Review of Linguistics, 1977, 2 (2):57-64.

Ball C N. It-clefts and th-clefts[C]. Paper read at the LSA summer meeting, Champaign-Urbana, Ill,1978.

Baumann S. Information structure and prosody: Linguistic categoriesfor spoken language annotation[J]. ethods in empirical prosody research, 2006, 3: 153-180

Belletti A. Answering with a "cleft": The role of the null subject parameter and the VP periphery [C]. Proceedings of the Thirtieth "Incontro di Grammatica Generativa". Veneza: Cafoscarina, 2005: 63-82.

Benincà P. Son tre ore che ti aspetto [J]. Rivista di Grammatica Generativa, 1978 (3): 231–245.

Berruto G. Sociolinguistica dell'italiano contemporaneo [M]. Roma: Carocci, 1987.

Biber D, Johansson S, Leech G, et al. Longman grammar of spoken and written English (Vol. 2) [M]. Cambridge: MIT Press, 1999.

Bolinger D. English prosodic stress and Spanish sentence order [J]. Hispania,1954 (37): 152-156.

Büring D, Križ M. It's that, and that's it! Exhaustivity and homogeneity presuppositions in clefts (and definites)[J]. Semantics and Pragmatics, 2013, 6(6):1-29.

Bussmann H. Routledge dictionary of language and linguistics[M]. London: Routledge, 2000.

Brunetti L. Aunification of focus[M]. Padova: Unipress, 2004.

Calude A S. Demonstrative clefts in spoken English [D]. University of Auckland, 2007.

Cassarà A, Aria A, Karssemberg L. Clefts in context: A QUD-perspective on c'est/il ya utterances in spoken French. Isogloss. Open Journal of Romance Linguistics, 2002, 8(1): 1-29.

Chafe W. Givenness, contrastiveness, definiteness, subjects and topics[M]// Charles Li. Subject and topic. Academic Press,1976: 25-56.

Chafe W L. Cognitive constraints on information flow[M]// Tomlin R S. Coherence and Grounding in Discourse. Amsterdam: Benjamins, 1987:21-51.

Chafe W L. Discourse, consciousness, and time: The flow and displacement of conscious experience in speaking and writing[M]. University of Chicago Press, 1994.

Chao Y R. A grammar of spoken Chinese[M]. Berkeley and Los Angeles: University of California Press, 1968.

Cheng L L S. Deconstructing the shi ... de construction[J]. The Linguistic Review, 2008, 25(3-4): 235-266.

Cheng L L S, and Sybesma R. Bare and not-so-bare nouns and the structure of NP[J]. Linguistic inquiry, 1999, 30(4): 509-542.

Chen P. Identifiability and definiteness in Chinese[J]. Linguistics, 2004, 42 (6): 1129-1184.

Chierchia G, S McConnell-Ginet. Meaning and Grammar[M]. Mass: MIT Press, 1990.

Chiu Bonnie H-C. The inflectional structure of Mandarin Chinese [D]. University of California, Los Angeles, 1993.

Chomsky N. Some empirical issues in the theory of transformational grammar[M]// Chomsky, N. Studies on Semantics in Generative Grammar. The Hague: Mouton, 1972: 120-202.

Clark H H. Inferences in comprehension. Basic processes in reading: Perception and comprehension[M]. London: Routledge, 1977: 243-263.

Clech-Darbon A, Rebuschi G, Rialland A. Are there cleft sentences in French? [M]// Rebuschi and Tuller. The Grammar of Focus. Amsterdam: Benjamins, 1999: 83-118.

Collins, P. Cleft and pseudo-cleft sentences in English[M]. London: Routledge, 1991a.

Collins P. Pseudocleft and cleft sentences: a thematic and informational interpretation[J]. Linguistics, 1991b (29): 481–519.

Collins P. Cleft and pseudo-cleft constructions in English [M]. London: Routledge, 2002.

Cowles H W. The psychology of information structure[M]// Krifka M, Musan R. The Expression of Information Structure. Amsterdam: Benjamins, 2012 (5): 287-318.

De Cat C. French dislocation: Interpretation, syntax and acquisition[M]. New York: Oxford University Press, 2007.

De Cesare A M, Cleft constructions in a contrastive perspective. Towards an operational taxonomy[M]//Anna-Mria De Cesare. Frequency, From and Function of Cleft Constructions. Contrastive, Corpus-based Stud-ies. Berlin/Boston, De Gruyter, 2014: 9-48.

De Cesare A M, Garassino D, Marco R. A, et al. Form and frequency of Italian Cleft sentences in a corpus of electronic news: a comparative perspective with French, Spanish, German and English [M]//Anna-Maria De Cesare. Frequency, forms and functions of cleft constructions in Romance and Germanic: Contrastive, corpus-based studies. Berlin: De Gruyter Mouton, 2014: 49-99.

De Cesare A M, Cleft constructions in a contrastive perspective. Towards an operational taxonomy[M]//Anna-Maria De Cesare. Frequency, Form and Function of Cleft Constructions. Contrastive, Corpus-based Studies. Berlin/ Boston, De Gruyter, 2014: 9-48.

De Cesare A M, Garassino D. On the status of exhaustiveness in cleft sentences: An empirical and cross-linguistic study of English also-/on- ly-clefts and Italian anche-/solo-clefts[J]. Folia Linguistica, 2015, 49(1): 1-56.

Declerck R. Studies on copular sentences, clefts and pseudoclefts[M]. Leuven: Leuven University Press, 1988.

Delahunty G. The analysis of English cleft sentences[J]. Linguistic Analysis, 1984, 13 (2): 63-113.

Delin J. Properties of it-cleft presupposition[J]. Journal of Semantics,1992, 9 (4): 289-306.

Delin J, Oberlander J. Cleft sentences in context: Some suggestions for research methodology[D]. Ms., University of Stirling, 2005.

De Stefani E. Le strutture grammaticali come epifenomeni dell'interazione sociale? Riflessioni sull'uso delle costruzioni scisse nel parlato conversazionale italiano e francese[M]// Ferrari A. Sintassi storica e sincronica dell'italiano. Subordinazione, coordinazione, giustapposizione, vol. 3. Cesati, Firenze, 2009: 1617-1633.

Destruel E. The French c'est-cleft: An empirical study on its meaning and use[J]. Empirical Issues in Syntax and Semantics, 2012 (9): 95-112.

De Veaugh-Geiss, JS Tönnis, E Onea, et al. That's not quite it: An experimental investigation of (non-)exhaustivity in clefts [J]. Semantics and Pragmatics 2018 (11): 1-45.

Dik, Simon C. Studies in Functional Grammar[M]. London: Academic Press, 1980.

Dik, Simon C. The theory of functional grammar[M]. New York: Mouton de Gruyter, 1997.

Doetjes J, Rebuschi G, Rialland A. Cleft sentences[M]// Corblin F, De Swart H. Handbook of French semantics. Stanford: CSLI publications, 2004: 529-552.

Doherty M. Clefts in translations between English and German[J]. Target. International Journal of Translation Studies,1999, 11(2): 289-315.

Du Bois J W. Beyond definiteness: The trace ofidentity indiscourse[A]// Chafe WL, ed. The Pear Stories: Cognitive, Cultural. and Linguistic Aspects of Narrative Production. Norwood, NI: Ablex Publishing Corporation. 1980: 203-274.

Durrell M. Hammer's German grammar and usage 4th ed[M]. London: Arnold, 2002.

Dufter A. On explaining the rise of c'est-clefts in French [M]//Amsterdam Studies in the Theory and History of Linguistic Science, series IV. Amsterdam: John Benjamins Publishing Company, 2008, 293:31.

Dufter A. Clefting and discourse organization: Comparing Germanic and Romance[M]// Dufter A. Jacob D. Focus and background in Romance languages. Amersterdam: John Benjamins Publishing Company, 2009: 83-121.

Drubig H B. Toward a typology of focus and focus constructions [J]. 2003:1-50.

Engel U. Deutsche Grammatik[M]. München: Iudicium Verlag, 1988.

Enç M. The semantics of specificity. Linguistic Inquiry, 1991 (22): 1-26.

Epstein R. The Definite Article, Accessibility, and the Construction of Discourse Referents[J]. Cognitive Linguistics, 2002,12 (4): 333-378.

Firbas J. Non-thematic subjects in contemporary English[J]. Travaux linguistiques de Prague, 1966(2):239-256.

Fischer K. Cleft sentences: Form, function, and translation[J]. Journal of Germanic Linguistics, 2009, 21(2):167-191.

Fodor J D, Sag I A. Referential and QuantificationalIndefinites[J]. Linguistics and Philosophy, 1982 (5):355–398.

Frascarelli M. Ramaglia. (Pseudo) Clefts at the syntax-prosody-discourse interface[M]// Hartmann, K., Veenstra, T. Cleft Structure. Amsterdam: Benjamins, 2013: 97-140.

Fries P H. On the status of theme in English: arguments from discourse[C]. Micro and macro connexity of texts. Hamburg: Buske, 1983: 116-152.

Frison L. Alcune differenze tra L'inglese e l'italiano nel comportamento della frase scissa[J]. Rivista di Grammatica Generativa, 1982(7):79-121.

Frison L. Le frasi scisse[J]. Grande grammatica italiana di consultazione, 2001(1):208-239.

Garassino D. Using cleft sentences in Italian and English. A multifactorial analysis[M]// De Cesare, Anna-Maria Garassino D. Current issues in Italian, Romance and Germanic non-canonical word orders. Syntax–information structure–discourse function, 2016: 181-204.

Gazdar G. Pragmatics: Implicature, Presupposition, and Logical Form[M]. New York: Academic Press, 1979.

Ginzburg J. Interrogatives: Questions, facts and dialogue[M]// Lappin S Fox C. The Handbook of Contemporary Semantic Theory, Oxford: Blackwell publisher, 1996: 385–422.

Goodman E. Keeping in touch. New York: Summit Books, 1985.

Graffi G. On Italian cleft sentences[M]// Conte M E, Ramat A G, Ramat, P. Wortstellung unde Bedeutung. Akten des 12 Linguistischen Kolloquiums. Tübingen: Niemeyer, 1978: 113-123.

Grewendorf G, Poletto C. La costruzione scissa: un'analisi contrastiva[J]. Rivista di Grammatica Generativa, 1989 (14):105-142.

Grice H P. Logic and conservation[M]. Harvard: Harvard University Press, 1975.

Grice H P. Studies in the Way of Words[M]. Harvard: Harvard University Press, 1989.

Groenendijk J. The logic of interrogation[C]. Proceedings of SALT IX, 109–126. Ithaca, NY: Cornell University, 1999.

Gundel J K. Universals of topic-comment structure[M]// Hammond M, Moravsik E A, Wirth J. Studies in Syntactic Typology. Amsterdam: John Benjamin Publishing, 1988(17):209-239.

Gundel J K, Hedberg N, and Zacharski R. Cognitive status and the form of referring expressions in discourse[J]. Language,1993: 274-307.

Gundel J K, and Fretheim T. Topic and focus[M]// Horn L, Ward G. The handbook of pragmatics. MA: Blackwell Pub, 2004: 175-196.

Halliday M A K. Notes on theme and transitivity in English[J]. *Journal of Linguistics*, 1967, 3.

Halvorsen P K G. The syntax and semantics of cleft constructions[D]. Austin, TX: University of Texas, 1977.

Hamlaoui F. Focus, contrast and the syntax-phonology interface: The case of French cleft sentences[C]. Proceedings of the 18th International Congress of Linguists, 2008.

Hartmann K, Zimmermann M. Exhaustivity marking in Hausa: Areanalysis of nee/cee[A]//Aboh E, Hartmann K,Zimmermann M, eds. *Focus Strategies in Afican Languages*. Berlin: Mouton de Gruyter, 2007: 241-267

Hashimoto A Y. The verb 'to be' in Modemn Chinese[M]//The verb 'be' and its synonyms. Springer Netherlands, 1969: 72-111.

Hasegawa N. A Copula-based Analysis of Japanese Clefts: Wa-Cleft and Ga-Cleft[M]// Inoue K. Researching and Verifying an Advanced Theory of Human Language. COE: Kanda University of International Studies, 1997: 15-38.

Hawkins J A. On (in)definite articles: Implicatures and (un)grammaticality prediction[J]. Journal of Linguistics, 1991(27):405– 442.

Hedberg N. The discourse function of cleft sentences in spoken English[C]. Linguistic Society of America, 1988: 1-13.

HedbergN. Discourse pragmatics and cleft sentences in English[D]. Minneapolis: University of linnesota. 1990.

Hedberg N. The referential status of clefts[J]. Language,2000: 891-920.

Hedberg N. Multiple focus and cleft sentences[M]// Hartmann, K., Veenastra, T. Cleft Structures. Amsterdam: John Benjamins, 2013: 227-250.

Hedberg N. Fadden L, Wh-clefts and reverse wh-clefts in English[M]// Hedberg. N, Zacharski R, The Grammar Pragmatics Interface: Essays in Honor of Jeanette K. Gundel. Amsterdam: John Benjamins, 2007: 49-76.

Heim I R. The semantics of definite and indefinite noun phrases[D]. University of Massachusetts Amherst, 1982.

Heggie L. A unified approach to copular sentences[C]. Proceedings of WCCFL 7, 1988: 129-142.

Higgins, Francis R. The Pseudo-Cleft Construction in English[M]. London: Routledge, 1979.

Himmelmann N P. Demonstratives in narrative discourse: A taxonomy of universal uses[J]. Typological studies in language, 1996 (33):205-254.

Hiraiwa K, Ishihara S. Missing links: Cleft, sluicing, and "no da" construction in Japanese[C]. MIT Working Papers in Linguistics, 2002:(43) 35-54.

Hoji H. Japanese clefts and reconstruction/chain binding ef- fects[R]. Handout of talk presented at The West Coast Conference on Formal Linguistics, 1987:6.

Hoji H, Ueyama A. Resumption in Japanese[D]. Los Angeles: Uni- versity of Southern California, 1998.

Hole D. The deconstruction of Chinese shì … de clefts revisited[J]. Lingua, 2011,121(11): 1707-1733.

Hole D. The information structure of Chinese[M]. The Expression of Information Structure. Amsterdam: Benjamins, 2013: 45-70.

Horn L R. On the Semantic Properties of Logical Operators in English[D]. Los Angeles: University of California, 1972.

Horn L R. Exhaustiveness and the Semantics of Clefts[C]. Proceedings of the 11th Annual Meeting of the North Eastern Linguistic Society. Amherst: University of Massachusetts, 1981: 125-142.

Horn L R, and Bayer S. Short-circuited implicature: A negative contribution[J]. Linguistics and Philosophy, 1984,7(4): 397–414.

Huang C J. Move WH in a language without WH movement[J]. The Linguistic Review, 1982, 1(4): 369-416.

Huang C J. Existential sentences in Chinese and (in)definiteness. The representation of (in)definiteness. Cambridge: MIT Press, 1987:226-253.

Huang C J. Shuo 'shi' he 'you': jiantan zhongwen de dongci fenlei (A discussion of "be" and "have": with verb classification in Chinese)[D]. Cornell University, 1988.

Huang C J. Between syntax and semantics[M]. London: Routledge, 2010.

Huang G, Fawcett R P. A functional approach to two 'focussing' constructions in English and Chinese[J]. Language Sciences, 1996, 18(1): 179-194.

Huang Y. Anaphora[M]. Oxford: Oxford University Press, 2007.

Huang Y. The Oxford dictionary of pragmatics[M]. Oxford: Oxford University Press, 2012

Huang Y. Pragmatics [M]. 2 ed. Oxford: Oxford University Press, 2014.

Huddleston, R, Pullum G K. The Cambridge grammar of the English language[M]. Cambridge: Cambridge University Press, 2002.

Iemmolo G, Arcodia G F. Differential object marking and identifiability of the referent: A study of Mandarin Chinese[J]. Linguistics, 2014, 52(2): 315-334.

Jackendoff R. Semantic interpretation in Generative Grammar[M]. Cambridge: MIT Press, 1972.

Jacobs J. Syntax und Semantik der Negation im Deutschen[M]. München: Wilhelm Fink, 1982.

Jespersen O. A Modern English Grammar on Historical Principles, Part III: Syntax [M]. Heidelberg: Winter, 1927.

Jespersen O. Analytic syntax[M]. Chicago: University of Chicago Press, 1937

Jespersen O. A Modern English Grammar, Volume VII. London: Allen and Unwin, 1949.

Kamp H. A theory of truth and semantic representation[J]. Formal semantics — the essential readings, 1981: 277-322.

Karttunen L. Presuppositions of compound sentences[J]. Linguistic inquiry, 1973, 4(2): 169-193.

Katz S. The syntactic and pragmatic properties of the c'est-cleft construction[D]. The University of Texas at Austin, 1997.

Katz S. A functional approach to the teaching of the French c'est-cleft[J]. French Review, 2000: 248-262.

Keenan E L. On Semantically based grammar[J]. Linguistic Inquiry, 1972(3) 413-461.

Keenan E L. Formal semantics of natural language[M]. Cambridge: Cambridge University Press, 1975.

Kiss K É. Discourse configurational languages[M]. Oxford: Oxford University Press, 1995.

Kiss K É. Identificational focus versus information focus[J]. *Language*, 1998 (74):245-273.

Kizu M. Cleft sentences in Japanese syntax[M]. New York: Palgrave Macmillan, 2005.

Knowles J. The cleft sentence: a base-generated perspective[J]. Lingua, 1986, 69(4): 295-317.

Koizumi M. Phrase structure in Minimalist Syntax [D]. Massachusetts Institute of Technology, 1995.

Kripke S A. Presupposition and anaphora: Remarks on the formulation of the projection problem[J]. Linguistic Inquiry, 2009,4 0(3):367-386.

Kuno, S. The structure of the Japanese language[M]. Cambridge: MIT

Press, 1973.

Lambrecht K. Information structure and sentence form: Topic, focus, and the mental representations of discourse referents[M]. Cambridge: Cambridge University Press, 1994.

Lambrecht K. A framework for the analysis of cleft sentences[J]. Linguistics, 2001, (39): 463-516.

Lambrecht K. Constraints on subject-focus mapping in French and English: A contrastive analysis[M]//Breul C, Göbbel E. Comparative and contrastive studies of information structure. Amsterdam: Benjamins, 2010:77-100.

LaPolla R J. Topicalization and the question of lexical passives in Chinese[C]. Proceedings of the Third Annual Ohio State University Conference on Chinese Linguistics. Indiana University Linguistics Club, 1988 : 170-188.

LaPolla R J. Pragmatic relations and word order in Chinese[M]. Amsterdam: John Benjamins Publishing Company, 1995.

Lee H C. On de in shi ... de construction[C]. UST Working Papers in Linguistics, Graduate Institute of Linguistics 1. National Tsing Hua University, 2005.

Lees R B. Analysis of the "Cleft Sentence" in English[J]. STUF-Language Typology and Universals, 1963, 16(1-4): 371-388.

Leopold W. Polarity in language [M]// Curme volume of linguistics studies, Baltimore, Waverly Press,1930:102-109

Levinson S C. Presumptive Meanings: The theory of generalized conversational implicature[M]. Cambridge: MIT Press, 2000.

Li C, Thompson S. Mandarin Chinese: A functional reference grammar. Berkeley: University of California Press, 1981.

Li K. Contrastive focus structure in Mandarin Chinese[C]. Proceedings of the 20th North American Conference on Chinese Linguistics (NACCL-20) (Vol. 2) 2008: 759-774.

Li Y, Sun J, Zhou G, et al. Complex sentence relative recognition and classification based on Tsinghua Chinese Treebank[J]. Acta Scientiarum Naturalium Universitatis Pekinensis 2014, 50(1): 118-124.

Longobardi G. Reference and proper names[J]. *Linguistic Inguiry*, 1994, 25: 609-666.

Lyons J. Semantics: Volume 2[M]. Cambridge: Cambridge University Press, 1977.

Lyons C. Definiteness[M]. Cambridge: Cambridge University Press, 1999.

Martinet A. Économie des changements phonétiques: traité de phonologie diachronique. Berne: Francke, 1955.

Mathesius V. Zur satzperspektive im modernen Englisch[J]. Archiv für das Studium der neueren Sprachen und Literaturen, 1929, 155(29): 202-210.

McCawley J D. Presupposition and discourse structure[M]// Oh C K, Dinneen D A. Syntax and Semantics, Volume 11: Presupposition. New York: Academic Press, 1979: 371–388.

McCawley J D. Actions and events despite Bertrand Russell[M]// Sinnott-Amstrong, W. Actions and Events. Perspectives on the Philosophy of Donald Davidson. Oxford: Basil Blackwell, 1985: 177–192.

Metzeltin M. La scissione relativa in italiano e nelle altre lingue romanze[M]// F Foresti, E Rizzi, P Benedini (a c. di). L'italiano fra le lingue romanze. Roma: Bulzoni, 1989: 151–169.

Miller J. Clefts, particles and word order in languages of Europe[J]. Language Sciences, 1996, 18(1-2):111–125.

Miller J. Subordination in spoken discourse[M]// Brown K. Encyclopaedia of Language and Linguistics, 2nd edition. Cambridge: Elsevier Press, 2006: 255–257.

Morgan J. Two types of convention in indirect speech acts[M]// Pragmatics, Brill, 1978: 261-281.

Niimura M. A syntactic analysis of copular sentences[J]. Nanzan Linguistics: Special Issue, 2007, 1(3): 203-237.

Noonan M. Woock E B. The passive analog in Lango[C]. Annual Meeting of the Berkeley Linguistics Society: Vol.4, 1978: 128-139.

Paul W, Whitman J. Shi ... de focus clefts in Mandarin Chinese[J]. The Linguistic Review, 2008, 25(3-4): 413-451.

Pavey E. An analysis of it-clefts within a Role and Reference Grammar framework[C]. University of North Dakota Working Papers, 2003: 47.

Percus O. Prying open the cleft[C]. North East Linguistic Society (NELS), 1997 (27): 337–351.

Poutsma H. A Grammar of Late Modern English: the elements of the sentence[M]. Groningen: P. Noordhoff, 1928.

Prince E F. A comparison of wh-clefts and it-clefts in discourse[J]. Language, 1978: (54) 883–906.

Prince E F. Topicalization, focus-movement, and Yiddish-movement: a pragmatic differentiation[C]. Annual meeting of the Berkeley Linguistics Society, 1981 (7): 249-64.

Quirk R, S Greenbaum, G Leech J, et al. A comprehensive grammar of the English language[M]. London: Longman, 1985.

Reinhart T. Pragmatics and linguistics: An analysis of sentence topics [J]. Philosophica, 1981, 27(1): 53-94.

Roberts C. Information structure in discourse: Toward a unified theory of formal pragmatics[C]. Ohio State University Working Papers in Linguistics, 1996 (49): 91-136.

Rochemont M S. Focus in generative grammar (Vol. 4) [M]. Amsterdam: John Benjamins Publishing Company, 1986.

Roggia C E. Le frasi scisse in italiano. Struttura informativa e funzioni discorsive[M]. Genève: Slatkine, 2009.

Ross C. On the functions of Mandarin de+ Chinese de as an NP and adverbial modification marker in prenominal strings, including cleft and equational structures[J]. Journal of Chinese Linguistics, 1983, 11(2): 215-246.

Sabatini F. "L'italiano dell'uso medio": una realtà tra le varietà linguistiche italiane[M]// Holtus, G. Gesprochenes Italienisch in Geschichte und Gegenwart. Tübingen: Narr, 1985: 154–184.

Searle J. Indirect speech acts[M]// Cole P, Morgan J. Syntax and semantics, volume 3: Speech acts. New York: Academic Press, 1975: 59-82.

Selkirk E. Contrastive FOCUS vs. presentational focus: Prosodic evidence from right node raising in English.[C] Speech Prosody, international conference, 2002.

Sgall P, Hajicova E E. Benesova. Topic, Focus and Generative Semantics. Kronberg: Taunus, 1973.

Shibatani M. Passives and related constructions: a prototype analysis[J]. Language 1985 (61):821-848.

Shi D. The nature of Chinese emphatic sentences[J]. Journal of East Asian Linguistics,1994, 3(1): 81-101.

Simpson A, Wu X Z Z. The syntax and interpretation of sentence-final DE[C]. Proceedings of North Amercian Conference on Chinese Linguistics, 1999 (10): 257-274.

Smith C S, Erbaugh M S. Temnporal interpretation in mandarin chinese[J]. 2005.

Sornicola R. Origine e diffusione della frase scissa nelle lingue romanze (vol. 3) [M]. Max Niemeyer Verlag, 1991: 43-54.

Stalnaker R C. Presuppositions[J]. Journal of Philosophical Logic, 2, 1973: 447-457.

Stowell T. Subjects, specifiers, and X-bar theory[A]//Baltin M R, KrochA S, eds. *Altenative Conceptions ofPhrase Stuctre*. Chicago: University of Chicago Press, 1989: 232-262.

Strawson P. Identifying reference and truth-value[J]. Theoria, 1964, 30(2): 96-118.

Sudo Y. Presupposition[M]// Oxford Bibliographies in Linguistics. Oxford: Oxford University Press, 2014.

Sunakawa Y. Nihongo ni okeru bunretsubun no kinou to gojun no genre[M]// Sunakawa Y. *Fukkubun no Kenkyu*. II. Tokyo: Kuroshio Shuppan, 1995: 353-388.

Sweet H. A history of English sounds from the earliest period: with full word-lists[M]. Oxford: Clarendon Press, 1888.

Szabolcsi, A. Compositionality in focus[J]. Folia Linguistica, 1981,15(1-2): 141-162.

Tang S W. Nominal predication and focus anchoring [A]//Jager G, Strigin A, Wilder C, Zhang N, eds. ZAS Papers in Linguistics. Berlin: ZAS, 2001: 159-172.

Teng S H. Remarks on cleft sentences in Chinese. Journal of Chinese-Linguistics[J]. 1979, 7(1): 101-114.

Takahashi D. Apparent parasitic gaps and null arguments in Japanese[J]. Journal of East Asian Linguistics, 2006, 15(1): 1-35.

Van Valin R D. A typology of the interaction of focus structure and syntax[M]// Raxilina E, Testelec J. Typology and Linguistic Theory: From Description to Explanation. Moscow: Languages of Russian Culture, 1999: 511-24.

Van der Sandt R. A. Presupposition and discourse structure[M]//van Emde Boas P, Barsche R, van Benthem J. Foris: Semantics and Contextual Expression, 1989 (11):278-294.

Whitney W D. The principle of economy as a phonetic force[J]. Transactions of the American Philological Association (1869-1896), 1877, 8: 123-134.

Zhan F, Traugott E C. The development of the Chinese copula shì construction: A diachronic constructional perspective[J]. Functions of Language, 2019, 26(2): 139-176.

Zifonun G, Hoffmann L, Strecker, B. Grammatik der deutschen Sprache (Vol. 1) [M]. Walter de Gruyter, 1997.

Zipf G K. Human behavior and the principle of least effort[M]. Cambridge: Addison-Wesley Press, 1949.

In Memory of Professor Yan Huang

This book is dedicated to my Ph.D. supervisor, Professor Yan Huang. Without his careful guidance and unwavering support, this work would not have been possible.

A globally renowned linguist, Professor Huang was known for his unwavering pursuit of knowledge, sharp critical thinking, and lifelong dedication to academic research. He exemplified academic excellence and served as a lasting inspiration for generations of scholars.

As a supervisor, his profound intellectual passion and meticulous scholarly attitude served as a beacon, guiding his students through the complexities of research and discovery.

Professor Huang passed away in 2022, leaving a great loss to the field of linguistics. As one of his Ph.D. students, I remain deeply influenced by his intellectual legacy and will continue to draw inspiration from his academic spirit throughout my career.

Zheng Danyang
August 2023
Tianjin University, China